Disability, Policy and Professional Practice

This book is dedicated to our colleagues and friends in the UK Disabled People's Movement, to our colleagues at the Universities of Dundee and Northumbria University, to our co-Executive Editors at *Disability and Society* journal and in particular to Professor Len Barton, the Editor in Chief, who recently retired after a long and distinguished career in Disability Studies and Inclusive Education.

We wish to thank all our colleagues, friends and families for their patience whilst we wrote this book and for their encouragement.

Disa...bility Policy and
Prof...ice

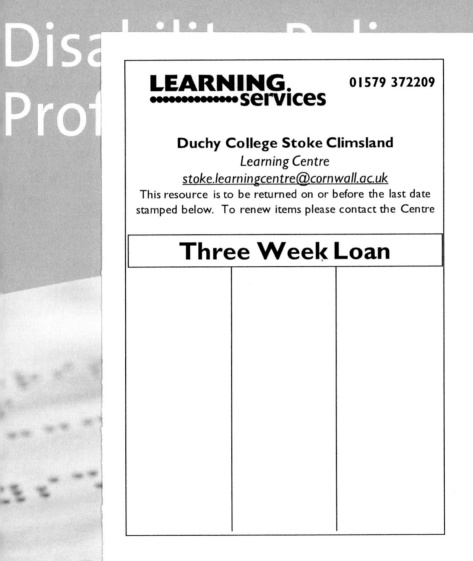

SAGE

Los Angeles | London | New Delhi
Singapore | Washington DC

SAGE Publications Ltd
1 Oliver's Yard
55 City Road
London EC1Y 1SP

SAGE Publications Inc.
2455 Teller Road
Thousand Oaks, California 91320

SAGE Publications India Pvt Ltd
B 1/I 1 Mohan Cooperative Industrial Area
Mathura Road
New Delhi 110 044

SAGE Publications Asia-Pacific Pte Ltd
33 Pekin Street #02-01
Far East Square
Singapore 048763

Library of Congress Control Number: 2010927595

British Library Cataloguing in Publication data

A catalogue record for this book is available from the British Library

ISBN 978-1-84920-169-8
ISBN 978-1-84920-170-4 (pbk)

Typeset by C&M Digitals (P) Ltd, Chennai, India
Printed by MPG Books Group, Bodmin, Cornwall
Printed on paper from sustainable resources

Mixed Sources
Product group from well-managed
forests and other controlled sources
www.fsc.org Cert no. SA-COC-1565
© 1996 Forest Stewardship Council

Contents

1

Introduction

There has never been a more interesting time to study the convergence of disability with social policy and professional practice. This book distils the many and various legislative and policy changes that have occurred over successive years since the inception of the welfare state to the present into a readable form for both practitioners and students working with disabled people.

Disability studies is an evolving discipline, largely borne from the discontent of members of the Disabled Peoples Movement, allied academics and professionals with traditional forms of health and social care services that have served to individualise disabled people's issues and consequently produce isolating forms of service provision. This book seeks to demonstrate how disabled people and their allies have undertaken a journey from a time when they and their services were *shaped* by legislators and policy makers, to the present time when disabled people have turned the tables and are now participating in the *shaping* of disability policy.

With this new shaping possibility, has come the requirement to rethink modes of working with disabled people. Traditional service forms based on 'expert power' wielded by cohorts of unenlightened professionals are no longer relevant in this new era. There is a pressing need instead for new forms of practice such as those described here, based on facilitation and advocacy and acknowledging the primacy and centrality of service users' choice and control. Such practice should be personalised and outcome-focused. There is a unique defining moment here for professionals involved with disabled people to utilise their professional skills to support, facilitate and advocate for disabled people in a new form of *positive practice* described in this book.

Disabled people have in modern times had an increasingly fraught relationship with 'professionals' from Health and Social Services – the 'caring professions'. We aim to show in this book that many if not all of these issues have been either directly or indirectly caused by adherence to the individual model of disability

(Oliver, 1990), inappropriate and unwieldy bureaucratic structures and an obsession with expert power, at the expense of focusing on disabled people's requirements. Although many disabled people and commentators have bemoaned this situation (Davis in Swain et al., 2004), little by way of solution has been suggested.

It is widely thought that professionals that act in these ways are unhelpful, that the lack of choice (Davis, in Swain et al., 2004) that is endemic in traditional service provision is lamentable and that basically everything takes too long owing to the creaking top-heavy structures in place, but very few acceptable suggestions and models of professional practice have been put forward by disabled people and their allies. Yet these pockets of non-stigmatising, helpful and assistive models and practice do exist, albeit in isolated and not well publicised formats (Harris et al., 2005; Silburn in Swain et al., 2004). It is an aim of this book to capitalise on these models and frameworks in order to demonstrate that assistance can be provided in ways that allow for choice and control to be retained and that are based on relationships of equality and respect. The term 'professional practice' in our title therefore, does not reflect an endorsement of professional statuses, traditional service provision or 'expert power'; in fact the opposite. Instead we seek to both problematise the concept and explore the tenets of (what we term as) 'positive practice' – ways of working with disabled people to achieve the desired outcomes of choice.

Importantly and centrally, this book is written by two allies of the British Disabled Peoples Movement who take their perspective from the social model of disability:

> For many years doctors, social workers and other people have told disabled people that they are disabled because of 'what is wrong with them' – their legs don't work, they can't see or hear or they have difficulty learning things, just to give a few examples. This is known as the medical model of disability. It says that it is the person's 'individual problem' that they are a disabled person.
>
> What we say is that yes, we do have bits of us that don't work very well, this we call our impairment: for example a person who cannot hear very well has a hearing impairment. What we say is that it is not this impairment which makes us a disabled person, it is society which makes us disabled. Society does not let us join in properly – information is not in accessible formats, there are steps into buildings, people's attitudes towards us are negative. So society puts barriers before us which stop us from taking part in society properly – it disables us. This is known as the social model of disability. (Greater Manchester Coalition of Disabled People, Young Disabled People's Group, 1996; quoted in Morris, 1999: 5)

Thus the social model of disability (Oliver, 1990) is far more than a guiding principle, it is a political commitment that informs and directs action. Much is written in this book about the social model of disability; its aims and reach and the pervasive and profound ways in which it has altered the public consciousness concerning disability and impairment.

Positive practice, as described here, is firmly rooted in the social model of disability and the 'seven needs' (information; access; housing; technical aids; personal assistance; counselling; and transport) (Harris et al., 2005; Silburn in Swain et al., 2004).

Throughout this book, we use the term 'disabled people' in a social model of disability sense – to refer to people disabled and/or oppressed by the majority society of non-disabled people. In the majority of the discussions below, we do not distinguish disabled people on the grounds of individual impairment types, except when discussing service silos set up for particular groups.

In setting out the stall for positive practice, we aim to influence a new generation of workers who will be involved in disabled people's lives. Whilst much of the bedrock of positive practice is philosophical therefore, we aim to show that working positively with disabled people is equally about personal attitude and political commitment to the goals and outcomes of the Disabled Peoples Movement. It is assumed that professionals will wish to develop such positive attitudes through direct experience and through an ongoing willingness to learn from disabled people and a willingness to pass this on to colleagues. Only in this way will new forms of assistance flourish.

We wrote this book because we were concerned that very few authors (especially within disability studies) appear to write about positive ways of working with disabled people and yet the statutory system of Health and Social Care, as well as housing, employment and training, is full of practitioners who do work every day with disabled people. Whilst it is comparatively easy to level criticism at service providers who fail to aspire to the high quality standards of service provision that disabled people rightly demand, it is more difficult to synthesise core messages of good practice that they can use to improve their work. However, such models do exist and we detail many of them here.

We realise that some people will say that a system that does not support the key areas of intent for disabled people is no use and should be disbanded and that perhaps our intention is merely to extol its continuation. However, we believe that the current system of statutory service provision in Health and Social Services will continue for the foreseeable future, most likely in a similar form, and for those disabled people who come into contact with professionals, it would be better if they are trained to be positive practitioners, using social model of disability principles, and positive methods such as outcome-based practice. While the statutory service system exists, let us have the best positive professionals that we can. We would like to see services that empower disabled people and that seek to assist them to achieve their desired outcomes, delivered by enlightened professionals who work to facilitate access to the resources that disabled people want and need. None of this is impossible, but it does take thought and a willingness to suspend disbelief.

The book is laid out in nine chapters which includes this introductory chapter and a Conclusion. In Chapter 2 we introduce the historical legacy, legislation and policy guidance that forms the bedrock of disability studies in the UK. In Chapter 3, 'Community Care and Beyond', we discuss the importance of community care and deinstitutionalisation as a turning point in both policy and service provision modes. In Chapter 4, we explore 'Pivotal Moments in the Development of Disability Policy', particularly those relating to the recent shift in consciousness that occurred when disabled people began to shape social policy. Thus we discuss the social model of disability, mainstreaming and balancing greater individual choice with resource equity, before exploring the lessons of history and the new demands in practice, positive practice and advocacy, facilitation and empowerment. Finally, we discuss the implications of Equality 2025 and the growth of Centres of Inclusive Living. In Chapter 5, 'Independent Living, Choices and Rights' we discuss enabling practice in the 21st century and key laws and policy guidance documents that underpin practice, including Working Futures; Direct Payments; Personalisation and Self-directed Support; Independence, Wellbeing and Choice; In Control and Individual Budgets.

This is followed by Chapter 6, 'Life Course Issues' which explores the issues that arise across the life course for disabled people, particularly for children. Hence we discuss Every Child Matters, Every Disabled Child Matters, disabled children's wheelchair services and transition from children's to adult services. We follow this with an examination of working with older disabled people; practice issues for adult social care and older people; home-based living options for disabled people; practice points with assistive technologies and the family context, in which we explore how to balance disabled people's rights with those of carers. In Chapter 7, 'Valuing Diversity' we explore mental health, learning disability, gender and disability, ethnicity, sexuality, sexual identity and parenting. All these issues form key learning points for the aspiring positive practitioner and the value bases that underlie them are important to examine reflexively.

In Chapter 8, 'Key Challenges for an Aspiring Social Model Practitioner' we examine the challenge of user choice and control and explore positive practice in more detail. We also look at 'managing the managers' and discuss budgetary constraints and street level bureaucracy – all factors which if unrecognised can lead to disempowerment by the system. The complex areas of 'mental capacity' and Power of Attorney are next examined, as is the issue of balancing different people's rights in practice. We then turn to working with colleagues in user-led organisations and discuss the opportunities for learning in practice from such working. Then we look at the possibilities for developing 'real reflexivity' in working with disabled people. In the Conclusion, we attempt to draw together the key lessons in this book for the positive practitioner.

Throughout this book you will find 'light bulb moments'. These are designed to get you thinking and often address issues to which there is no easy answer. Mostly, these issues are at the heart of professional practice dilemmas and concern ways in which practice can be improved. We suggest you consider the issues raised by these light bulb moments and write some notes on each one. As the issues in the main concern values and these differ between individuals, we suggest you engage others in discussing your notes. These could be supervisors, colleagues or others within your organisation. Given the interdisciplinary nature of disability studies and its situation between Health and Social Services (as well as the third sector) it would be really useful to discuss your notes with colleagues in these other sectors. Some issues may cause you concern and these are particularly worthy of note. Many professionals can appreciate good practice in an abstract sense but become uneasy and defensive when having to apply it in real life. It is worth making the effort to find some assistance or training on any issues that cause you concern. The chances are that these will form barriers to real reflexivity if not. As in so much of professional practice, there are no 'correct' answers.

2

The Historical Legacy, Legislation, Policy and Guidance

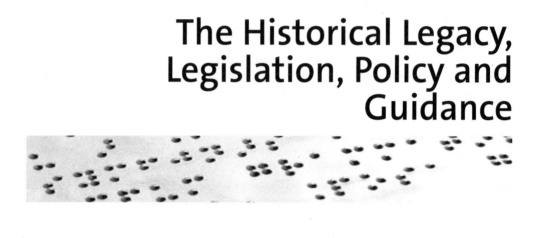

Introduction

In this chapter we critically explore the development of services and professional working with disabled people. The chapter aims to provide a policy and practice backdrop against which to understand the modernisation of disability services. The chapter also gives very strong clues as to the power of paternalism in disability services which originally underpinned much professional practice and which helps explain why despite apparently progressive new policies, the extent of improvement in services was often limited by the pre-existing ideas of professionals. Indeed early provision for disabled people was largely conditional upon accepting an enforced stigma for the protection received.

The roots of policy, legislation and protection

Throughout recorded history disabled people have seen decisions being made about their lives by those in 'authority' (Borsay, 2005). Interpretations of the functions of authority have varied. At times authority has been viewed as resting on straightforward power differentials and resulted in the imposition of practices designed to reaffirm the social marginalisation of disabled people (Barton, 2001; Finkelstein, 1980; Oliver, 1990). At other times the notion of authority has reflected the traditional professional view that disabled people as a population require social protection (Jay in Brechin et al., 1981). What connects these interventions is the history of legislative and policy developments that have helped legitimate the role of professional or expert interventions. It would be wrong however to suggest, as some authors (Davis, 1998) do, that most contemporary professional working with disabled people can trace its direct lineage back to guardians and relieving officers of the Poor Law system. The given matrix of economic and social forces that existed at any point in history has provided specific factors in shaping the nature of authorised support before the birth of named professionals – for example social workers, general practitioners, educational psychologists and occupational therapists. What we can say, however, with some degree of accuracy is that the broad shift throughout the last 500 years is best captured in the following typology:

- **Pre-industrialisation** – most disabled people were spatially integrated but often culturally excluded. Few authorised people existed to respond to disabled people. The Poor Law was the main form of support.
- **Industrialisation** produced large-scale shifts to institutionalisation of many disabled people. With late industrialisation a range of 'professionals' grew up to respond to the needs of disabled people
- The **decline of industrialised thinking** and growing humane sensibilities led to deinstitutionalisation for many, but not all disabled people. Professionals have been required officially to listen to disabled people's views as sensibilities towards difference alter in their favour. Arguably the very survival of some professions will require them to connect more fully with disabled peoples' perspectives.

Basic forms of voluntary and state-funded community and health support for disabled people were available before the key social legislations of the 1940s (Fraser, 2002; Lowe, 2005) and before the social care legislation of the 1970s. However, such support was haphazard, stigmatised and eligibility to a given form of support by definition marked a person out as different. The origins of the connection between stigma and disability can be found in the English Poor Law.

The Poor Law origins of health and social care

The English Poor Law was instituted in the reign of Elizabeth I in 1601. The recognition of the unmet needs of sick, infirm and disabled people although very basic and locally haphazard did afford basic protection for disabled people to at least survive alongside their non-disabled counterparts. Physical impairment, 'infirmity' and mental frailty all served as the basis of Poor Law support. The Poor Law however was designed with another express purpose – that of keeping 'the able bodied' away from local support. The Poor Law was targeted so as to not interfere with paid opportunities to work. It is interesting how if we come closer to date and look at social care, health and welfare policy in the 20th century that they are clearly treated separately. However it remains important to see where the divide is placed in terms of the welfare/work boundary as this helps position social and health care more generally. The Poor Law instituted in 1601 allowed largely outdoor relief and thus did not bear the hallmarks of the Poor Law which followed, which was the 1834 Poor Law Reform Act. In response to what can be described as an early form of 'welfare tourism' and the phenomenon of the 'sturdy beggar' able to hoodwink Poor Law guardians into support, the Poor Law Reform Act redrew the lines between eligible and non-eligible populations. The Poor Law Reform Act, whilst not successful in abolishing outdoor relief, did manage to push through a major ideological shift towards seeing welfare and support as not simply distinct from paid work, but as inherently *less eligible* than such work. Poor Law workers and guardians saw the legitimate users of the workhouse and indoor relief as 'paupers, children, the sick, insane, defective and the aged/infirm' (HM Government, 1834). Disability and institutionalisation became synonymous in the popular imagination. The workhouse, although on paper a 'protective environment', symbolised a threat to non-disabled people, a reminder of what might befall them if they failed to work hard. This in retrospect seems punitive on the legitimate users of Poor Law provisions and arguably the stigma attaching to social welfare and support seems to have pervaded much provision through to the present day.

Disabled people, abnormal bodies and industrialisation

A number of writers (Foucault, 1961; Oliver, 1990; Roulstone, 2002) have suggested that industrialisation and the Poor Law Reform Act confirmed the two populations of work: abled and disabled. Indeed Foucault points out the notion of abled and disabled would not otherwise make sense outside of the thinking attached to the new industrial logic of the factory system. Relatedly, Johnson argued that many of the officials founding the principles of the early industrial welfare state were progressing their professional projects on the back of the ideological project of confirming their knowledge as the new science of health and welfare (Johnson, 1977). Whether one accepts this argument or not, it is clear that the institutional provision embodied in the workhouses and large industrialised asylums helped forge the link between disability, abnormality and 'problem populations' (Davis, 1998; Stone, 1984).

As Finkelstein (1993) points out, disabled people both in institutions and those outside receiving what was often dubbed a 'home cure' were subject to the administrative model of disability, one that saw disabled people as being a dependent population needing professional support due to their inability to cope with mainstream life. The administrative model is simply an expanded version of the medical model of disability in assuming that professional help was needed because of the deficits and inabilities of disabled people. As he points out:

'Historically, professional intervention "confirms" the inherent passivity and dependence of disabled people, that disabled people cannot do certain things ... and therefore we intervene to help' (Finkelstein in Brechin et al., 1981).

Foucault (2001) took the comparison between factory and asylum one step further, noting that the new 'medical gaze' attaching to psychiatry closely mirrored the logic of industrial discipline and the disciplining institution. Foucault found surprising similarities between the panopticon principles of factory life, prisons and asylums and postulated that they all took their cue from the logic of indus-trialisation. The power of Foucault's analyses has been disputed. However what was unarguably correct was the idea held by many critical commentators that the logic of the factory system served to create dependency amongst a number of disabled people formerly very much at the centre of economic and social produc-tion (Finkelstein, 1980; Gleeson, 1999; Oliver, 1990; Roulstone, 2002). Contrary to a growing popular belief that disabled peoples' institutionalisation was entirely the result of limited capacity, Ryan and Thomas (1987) remind us that the nature of industrialised working epitomised in the factory system, served to exclude people whose bodies or brains were not 'industry standard'. We can see how a whole category of people was inadvertently excluded from such key forms of life where work provides economic survival and social citizenship, as Ryan and Thomas point out: 'The speed of factory life, the enforced discipline, the time-keeping and production norms – all these were a highly unfavourable change from the slower, more self determined and flexible methods of work into which many handicapped people had been integrated' (Ryan and Thomas, 1987: 181).

The categorical 'solution' to the 'problem of disabled people'

Whilst these analyses can be seen to be at times overly schematic (Borsay, 2005; Roulstone, 2002), they do hold a great deal of explanatory value in understand-ing the shape and pattern of welfare provision in the late 19th early 20th centu-ries. Empirical study of the workhouse system pointed to an increasing specialisation of workhouse populations based on often crude appraisals of 'disability', as Anne Crowther notes:

> Specialized institutions appealed to humanitarians who felt that the helpless would be 'better off' inside them; to eugenicists who hoped incarceration would prevent the unfit from breeding; to the medical elite who were themselves becoming more spe-cialized; and to a vague public sense of propriety who disliked mixing the deserving with the disreputable poor. (Crowther cited in Borsay, 2005: 32)

The years 1871–1901 witnessed a continued rise in the number of disabled people in workhouses, with often invidious distinctions being made between the deserving and non-deserving, with outdoor relief becoming harder to access for those disabled people who were not as visibly impaired as those who were blind or limbless (Borsay, 2005: 32).

By the end of the 19th century, well developed (if at times questionable) categorical approaches had been put in place to 'allocate' disabled people to types of services. In some instances being disabled meant no access at all, for example contrary to Forster's proposed universal Elementary Education Act 1875, physically disabled people often received little education as educational environments were inaccessible or the protective impulse attached most closely to young deaf or blind children who needed the most urgent forms of 'social rescue'. Many physically disabled children received what was euphemistically called a 'home cure' which essentially meant being reliant on family for support and social interaction (Barnes, 1991). Conversely much educational provision was established by church or charitable foundations and catered for 'blind, deaf, delicate, epileptic, and the feeble minded' (Adams, 1986).

In the late 19th century disabled children were seen as a liability in the mainstream as schools were often paid by results (Fulcher, 1989) and this disincentivised the enrolment of disabled children. Meanwhile the popularity of Francis Galton's views on eugenics and moral hygiene added impetus to the segregation of what became known as the 'feeble minded' and who presented an apparent moral threat to the 'healthy gene pool'. Together, payment by results and eugenics gave further impetus to the growth of segregated schooling. By 1899 a further Elementary Education Act was introduced explicitly for epileptic or 'defective' children. Pupils were eligible if 'by reason of mental or physical defect [they] are incapable of receiving benefit from the instruction in ordinary schools but are not incapable by reason of such defect of receiving benefit from instruction in special classes or schools'. Whilst there is no doubt that some children would be better nourished and educated in charitable and church schools given their parents' financial position, the low expectations of many schools helped cement the view that disability equated to inability. The fashion for Binet and Simon's fixed notions of intelligence encapsulated in IQ (intelligence quotient) added to the sense of what Ryan and Thomas (1980) called IQ fatalism which further solidified low expectations of disabled children. Even where protective impulses were more in evidence than those of moral hygiene, the result was lamentably similar as the following quote from the then Principal of Donaldson School for the Deaf (Edinburgh, 1890) suggests: 'In open society deaf children are the butt and gibe of their associates' (Adams, 1986).

Professionals at this time, whatever their view of disability and personal humanity, were wedded to the idea that disabled people are categorically *different* to non-disabled people. This assumption, although much challenged, still remains in much health, welfare and education thinking.

The Charity Organisation Society

The Charity Organisation Society, a London-based organisation, can be viewed as a key influence on the development of social work. Founded in 1869 by a group of respected reformers, the COS aimed to better coordinate charitable works with poor and marginalised people, many of whom would meet a contemporary definition of disability. The COS perspective can be gleaned from the following quote:

> It was the human weakness of the social workers that was often to blame. Without training, and often without adequate preparation regarding the aims and purposes of the society they served, these good-hearted, somewhat sentimental workers all to often were taken in by apparent distress that they tended to give relief as a matter of course. This put the best view on lack of discrimination, but less worthy motives were sometimes ascribed to them. It was said, for instance, that some churches competed with each other in gifts of soup and food tickets, in order to increase their congregations; that such was the competition among the relief societies working with the homeless that John Burns decided to clear the Thames Embankment of all charitable societies distributing relief there. (Young and Ashton, 1956: 93)

This view underplays the importance of the relief provided and whilst criticised for having a corrective moral crusading approach the COS was a key organisation in challenging the effects (if not the cause) of unbridled competition. Adams provides a slightly different critique of analyses of the COS, noting how writings overlook the more egalitarian approach of the provincial social guilds which were also active in combating poverty and distress (Adams et al., 2002: 332). Whichever view one takes, the COS can be criticised for tackling only the results of industrial capitalism and not its inner logic. However, it would be churlish to overlook the important and symbolic work undertaken. A more reasonable criticism does attach to the moralistic underpinnings of the COS and contemporary parallels are seen in criticisms of missionary activity by majority world countries.

The great confinement

Perhaps the most stark legacies to shape disabled peoples lives since industrialisation was the growth of asylums and long-stay hospitals. The asylum system remained a patchwork quilt of private and charitable funded provision until the mid-1850s when the building programme began for the large-scale 'county asylums'. The Lunacy Act of 1845, although imperfect, was a watershed in improvements of much asylum provision. Whilst conditions gradually improved with better inspection regimes (Borsay, 2005: 73), the larger institutions although more sanitary and generally improving, more closely resembled the Panopticon principles described by Foucault (1961) and became increasingly intolerant of difference (Digby, 1985)

In terms of long-term segregated residency the Mental Deficiency Act (1913) provided the blueprint for the use of categorical approaches to legitimise incarceration and justification for segregating those who were deemed to pose a threat to the gene pool. Inmates were given a range of negative descriptors ranging from idiots to moral defectives depending on the perceived level of threat. Many of these long-stay institutions lumped together people suffering with what was then uncritically called mental illness with those with mental handicaps.

The outrage in some quarters at the unplanned effects of industrialised life (not simply industry but the way the population lived more generally) led to the Liberal reforms of 1911 and the first attempt to insure individuals via the 1911 National Insurance Act. These reforms reflected concerns about the unchecked impact of industrialism and industrial capitalism. Voices began to be raised in the cause of women's suffrage. This was an age of rapid change – in a sense, both progressive and regressive. Working against the more progressive thrust of policy were the now largely discredited views of the psychologist and champion of IQ Cyril Burt. In 1913, Burt founded educational psychology. At the heart of this new profession was the perceived value of IQ and its categorical importance in allocating children to the 'correct' educational environment. IQ was presented amongst early educational psychologists as the science of human intellectual development and until the 1940s educational psychologists were the lead professional in many aspects of disabled peoples' education.

Somewhat ironically, the First World War (1914–18) acted as a positive (if unplanned) benefit for disabled adults. The numbers of war-injured and growing sensibilities attached to human loss aided both the entry of disabled people into selective wartime occupations, but also spawned the establishment of the Kings Roll, an early quota system for disabled peoples' employment representation. Although never achieving long-term changes in attitudes towards disabled people, this policy symbolised recognition of disabled peoples' abilities that had previously been held back in a world of segregation and low expectation (Humphries and Gordon, 1992).

Although there was a minimal legislative base for supporting disabled people, an exception was the legislation passed in response to the actions of the National League for the Blind and Disabled (NLBD). The NLBD had since the late 1890s been lobbying for support to aid blind peoples' entry to work. This culminated, some 30 years later, in the Blind Persons Act of 1920. This and subsequent Acts aimed to support the entry of blind and later deaf people into segregated workshops. These were philanthropic gestures, but they relied upon charitable provision of workshops and perpetuated the 'categorical' approaches to disability that discounted many from systems of support.

The two world wars and the rise of disability as a 'unified' policy category

The first piece of legislation to present disabled people as a discernible population was the Disabled Persons Employment Act. Passed in 1944, the Act was formulated following the recommendations of the Tomlinson Committee Report. Although many remember the Act for its development of the employment quota system (Thornton and Lunt, 1995), the Act is important in going beyond a divisive categorical approach to disability and in assuming that many disabled people could work alongside their non-disabled peers. The following extract from the Report symbolises a new way of viewing disability beyond that of problem populations:

> The successful rehabilitation of a person disabled by injury or sickness is not solely a medical problem and that close co-operation between the Health and Industrial services is necessary throughout the whole process ... Ordinary employment is the object and is practicable for the majority of the disabled, with the goodwill and co-operation of the representative organisations of employers and work people, in conjunction with the Health services and the responsible Government Departments. (Tomlinson Report, 1943:23)

The Tomlinson Report and the Act that followed, although never realised in full (Barnes, 1991), was an early example of the attempt to link up health, social and employment professionals and to acknowledge that disabled peoples' needs are not fragmented. This is therefore a precursor to later Acts which aimed, some 35 to 45 years later, to connect the facets of disabled peoples' lives that had been fragmented by the industrial system and the growing boundary making that often accompanies professionalisation.

As is so often the case in policy and practice terms, developments were also taking place which served to perpetuate the divisive and categorical approach to disability. Chief amongst these is the 1944 Education Act, the brainchild of the then education minister R.A. Butler. This Act is best remembered for ushering in the tripartite system of education and for its philosophy of education best suited to a child's 'ability, age and aptitude'. A less well known fact about the 1944 Act was its deliberate attempt to formulate a quasi-scientific categorisation of disability. This was captured in the (now heavily criticised) category of Educational Subnormality or ESN. The categories as defined by the Act were:

- Delicate/diabetic
- Epileptic
- Educationally subnormal (ESN)
- Children with mild/moderate sub normality
- Partially sighted
- Partially deaf

- Speech impaired
- Children with physical impairments
- Blind
- Deaf.

Perhaps the most disabling feature of the Act and its Guidance was the application of the term 'ineducable' to those children with 'severe mental handicaps' who were deemed educationally subnormal. These ideas drew on Cyril Burt's applications of IQ to disability and assisted in condemning some disabled children to little more than a warehousing approach (Miller and Gwynne, 1972). There were 'winners' and 'losers' from this categorisation process. Children with 'mild/moderate sub normality', partially sighted children, partially deaf and speech impaired were allowed where possible to be educated in the mainstream. Conversely blind, deaf, 'physically disabled' and epileptic children would ordinarily be educated in 'special school' contexts. The powerlessness of parents to reject the labels attached to their children was evident in the outcomes of the appeal process, with only four successful appeals registered out of 4,000 parental appeals between 1951 and 1960. The term 'ineducable' remained in common currency until it was overturned in the 1959 Mental Health Act.

During the 1940s, the only frontline social care professionals working with chronically sick and disabled people were hospital almoners, a prototype hospital social worker with roots in the charitable guild system that originally provided alms (charitable support) for disabled people. Hospital almoners helped make the link between hospital care (itself largely charitable or based on Poor Law support), community and family support. Prior to 1948, such work was not backed up with legislation or funding to provide support to disabled people leaving hospital.

The National Assistance Act 1948: an early precursor to community care

Whereas support for disabled people before industrialisation can technically be seen as community-based care, the notion of community support or care has been in more widespread use since World War Two to refer to more formalised and planned support for disabled and older people (Lowe, 2005). Strictly speaking, however, the term 'community care', although used in the Hospital Plan of 1961 was not in widespread use until the late 1980s. The Beveridge reforms encoded in the 1942 Report formed the blueprint for a new welfare state that would tackle the five giant evils: want, ignorance, idleness, disease and squalor. Although disability was not explicitly covered in these five evils, disabled people were disproportionately in evidence under many of these five headings. The architects of the 'New Jerusalem' soon realised that the contributory principle underpinning the new insurance-based welfare elements of the welfare state left those in greatest need unprotected. Those disabled and sick people who had never worked or were unlikely to be able to get paid work remained without support. This was the key driver behind the National Assistance Act (NAA) of 1948. Generally, community-based living had traditionally meant relying upon family or charity support before the advent of the welfare state and the National Assistance Act in 1948. The Act symbolised the winding up of the haphazard Poor Law that preceded it and empowered local authorities to register blind (who had been registered since 1920), deaf and physically disabled people to better gauge the service needs in a given locality. The National Assistance Act is best remembered for its continued faith in institutional provision for those deemed to have the greatest support needs. Section 21 of the NAA of course continued to emphasise institutional options for 'severely' disabled people whose 'deficits' were deemed 'permanent and substantial', a language that was carried forward into the 1970 Chronically Sick and Disabled Persons Act and is seen even as late as the Children Act of 1989 providing: ' … residential accommodation for persons aged eighteen or over who by reason of age, illness, disability or any other circumstances are in need of care and attention which is not otherwise available to them' (Section 21, National Assistance Act 1948).

The 1948 Act also committed to promoting the welfare of people over 18 years who were 'blind, deaf, dumb and other persons substantially and permanently handicapped by illness, injury or congenital deformity … ' (Section 29:1). Section 29 (4b & 4c) made reference to the use of workshops to provide suitable work for those able to undertake paid work or methods of instruction at home to help them 'overcome the effects of their disability'. The community basis for welfare support continued to be based on assumptions that disability was a problem that an individual had to overcome (see Chapter 3 below). The provision under the National Assistance Act 1948 ought not to be dismissed as this did represent at least some recognition, however limited, of the wider economic and social lives of disabled people. The categorical distinction between substantially disabled and not substantially disabled was, however, reaffirmed by the Act. Although sections of the 1948 Act are now repealed to bring it into line with later amending statutes, the Act remains an important piece of legislation in providing accommodation for some disabled people.

Towards community care

The more significant shift towards community-based social support for disabled people came with the Chronically Sick and Disabled Persons Act 1970 (CSDPA). Although still firmly within a paternalist model and drawing down entitlements from the earlier National Assistance Act, the Act emphasised community-based provision for a number of disabled people. The Act was in part a response to the growing evidence of the damaging and at times abusive nature of institutional living for many disabled people, as evidenced in the Ely, Farleigh and Normansfield hospital enquiries (DHSS, 1969, 1971; see also Miller and Gwynne, 1972; Morris, 1969), and of personal lobbying by influential commentators such as Alf Morris MP and Jack Ashley MP on the human cost of poor provision for disabled people both in and outside of institutions. These views represented a new sensibility towards disabled people which discussed disability in a less objectifying manner and a reading of parliamentary records for the time suggests early human rights thinking being applied to disabled people. Although these were minority voices, the future of large-scale institutions was beginning to be questioned, as here in the words of the then Minister of Health describing the vestige of Victorian asylums: 'There they stand, isolated, majestic, imperious, brooded over by the gigantic *water-tower* and chimney combined, rising unmistakable and daunting out of the countryside – the asylums which our forefathers built with such immense solidity to express the notions of their day' (Minister of Health, 1961).

With new developments in treatments for mental illness and changing sensibilities towards locking away people on the grounds of 'sub normality', clearly the writing began to appear on the wall for many of the larger long-stay institutions, as provision for mentally ill and 'mentally handicapped' people came under ever greater critical scrutiny. What in 21st-century terms seem rather paternalist views were, in the 1950s and 1960s, progressive shifts in thinking about difference amongst professionals. Jack Tizard, founder of the Tizard Centre suggested as early as 1952: 'Young feeble minded [sic] adults are the greatest single group in the mental deficiency hospitals. There seems no reason why most of them cannot be restored to the community after a period of education and training' (Tizard, 1954: 164, cited in Emerson, 2005). This assertion was backed up by psychological and sociological studies that made clear the potential for all disabled people to develop over the life course. The CSDPA captured the zeitgeist in emphasising community options. Section 1 of the CDSPA established that the number of disabled people needed to be established by local authorities in order to aid service delivery and ensure that needs were met. Section 2 of the Act laid out substantive provision that could be made and pertinently makes explicit the home as the focal point of service delivery. Broader social activities were also supported and although sounding morally improving in tone, they included 'provision for that person of lectures, games, outings and other recreational outings ... ' (Sec. 2(1)(c)). The establishment of the orange badge scheme in the Act symbolises the community-based focus of the CSDPA as the pre-existing Road Traffic Act (1968) was adjusted to afford disabled people access to otherwise restricted parking. Despite the symbolism of community and home the Act did not repeal the NAA 1948 and its emphasis on institutional 'options'; whilst the extent of local authority success in mapping local needs also failed to live up to the promise in the working of the Act, as the following quote from Alf Morris suggests:

There is obviously a wide chasm between the number of severely disabled people known to public authorities and the actual incidence of severe disablement. I ask the Minister, who I know to be very deeply concerned about the problems of disabled people, now to do everything he possibly can to see that the Section is implemented at the earliest possible date. (Hansard, *HC Deb*, 18 December 1970, vol. 808, cc1788–809)

Shortly after the CDSPA was placed on the statute book, the White Paper *Better Services for the Mentally Handicapped* was published. This added further impetus to the push towards community living options and to the closure of long-stay institutions. Whilst this did not mark the end of what were called 'Learning disability hospitals', it questioned their continued role. The CSDPA and *Better Services* White Paper did not signal the end of residential institutions, as can be seen from the debates between the Royal College of Physicians (1986) and their plan to build Young Disabled Units and a now growing number of vocal disabled people (Brisenden, 1986) willing to challenge the move. Between 1971 and 1985 some 58 'Young Disabled Units' (YDUs) were built to house those with more significant impairments decanted from or previously liable to enter large long-stay institutions. These units remained very medically focused and although the Units' 'patients' often had complex physical needs, their social needs ordinarily came way down the list of priorities in otherwise heavily medicalised environments. YDUs seemed anachronistic in an age of growing community provision and increased choices.

New voices for old ... new policy and practice visions   ● ● ● ● ● ●

The period 1970 to 1990 witnessed the rise of more radical and challenging disability organisations. Alongside the mainstream charities (RADAR, The Spastics Society, Disability Alliance and the Disablement Income Group), the Union of the Physically Impaired Against Segregation (UPIAS) was formed in 1975 to further the cause of a new social model of disability which placed the causes of disablement firmly at the door of an exclusionary society. Within this model, professionals were seen as part of the problem rather than a solution for disabled people in perpetuating disabled peoples' dependency. The writings of Vic Finkelstein and John McKnight in the late 1970s epitomised the call for professionals to decide whose side they were on (see Knight in Brechin et al., 1981). The watershed book *Handicap in a Social World* (Brechin et al., 1981) is testament to the changing professional landscape as the book contains chapters that clearly reflected both traditional and critical perspective on the role of professionals in the lives of disabled people. These works drew on the civil rights movement and thinkers of the late 1960s and borrowed ideas from other liberation struggles (Finkelstein, 1980).

Professionals for the first time were challenged not simply about the minutiae of practice issues, but more fully about their roles in relationship to disabled people. Notably, Finkelstein's famous three phase historical appraisal of the wider socio-economic treatment of disabled people, whilst critical of established professional relationships with disabled people, called not for a de-professionalisation process but for more enabling working between professionals and disabled people. In the field of formal education, Baroness Warnock's report of 1978 and the Education Act that followed in 1981 attempted to introduce new, less medicalised approaches to 'special education' by rejecting the ESN terminology that came out of the 1944 Education Act. It offered instead what were viewed as more universal categories that acknowledged that there existed a spectrum of abilities and that 'special needs', as they increasingly began to be called, attached to high achievers as much as to pupils with learning difficulties. The extent to which this destigmatised disabled children is questionable however (Barton, 2001; Tomlinson, 1982), especially as the segregated nature of such special schools helped cement mainstream views about difference. The term 'special educational needs' entered the popular vocabulary, but arguably the choices and rights of disabled children remained constrained by the low expectations and notions of difference that continued to attach to disabled children. As with most disability systems, disabled children and their families had to emphasise what they could not do in order to receive the highest levels of support, often via a Statement of Special Educational Needs.

The belief in the potential for professionals to work in an enabling way was built into the fabric of new Centres for Independent Living or CILs. The first, situated in Derbyshire, saw professionals supporting a range of projects and forums where professionals' roles were more clearly supporting disabled peoples' needs, both individually and collectively. Derbyshire Centre for Integrated Living opened in 1985 and worked with Derbyshire County Council to establish a CIL which combined traditional services with the '7 needs' identified by the UK Disabled Peoples' Movement. The CIL initiative saw early and largely successful attempts at joint statutory social services, health authority and disabled peoples' collaborative working. This emphasis on disabled people coming together to cohere around a broad agenda of choices and rights was a key moment in the history of disability policy and practice and although CILs have struggled to maintain their ambition in a difficult funding environment (Borsay, 2005), this move in the 1980s can be seen as symbolic of much broader shifts towards disabled people exercising choices and rights and also where preferred, to realise a collective identity in CIL settings. Despite these shifts, the number of disabled people able to avail themselves of CIL-type support remained very limited. Despite the impetus established in the Barclay Report (NISW, 1982) for social workers to better locate their practice in wider communities and community resource, many disabled people felt very much alone with the barriers and service issues they faced day-to-day (Bornat et al., 1993). Indeed the rhetorical shift towards choices and rights was well ahead of policy and practice level realities.

Policy remained firmly rooted in provider-led and often fixed modes of delivery. Assessment of 'needs' was often experienced as insensitive and fragmented, and at times entitlement formulae even within a given service seemed elusive.

Another development in policy and practice with disabled people was the passing of the Disabled Persons (Services, Consultation and Representation) Act 1986. This Act symbolised not simply the importance of choices for disabled people, but public recognition that disabled people should be consulted on and involved in the shaping of services. Most commentators establish that the 1986 Act although on paper a promising development has made little difference to the levels of consultation or representation (Barnes, 1991; Drake, 1999) beyond absolute statutory duties, for example the duty to transition plan for disabled children moving beyond school and from children's to adult services. The evidence from the 1980s suggests that the use of terms such as representation and consultation were both tentative and cursory in terms of going beyond formal recognition of the need to consult with disabled people and are perhaps best seen as more akin to 'keeping disabled people informed'. The road to real service choices, involvement and meaningful representation proved long. Of note, the major survey by Martin et al. (1989) which captured disabled peoples' lives in the mid 1980s showed no sign of disabled people receiving comprehensive services, with many disabled adults continuing to live in poverty (Oliver and Barnes, 1998: 40). Challenges continued to attach to joint working between health and social care authorities and the perception that professionals continued to provide those services they felt were appropriate for disabled people.

WHAT DO YOU THINK?

Who were the main 'gatekeepers' of resources and services for disabled people in the accounts given above?

What are the main assumptions that attached to disability in the above analysis?

Was it possible to work in an enabling way in this context?

How difficult was it for professionals and policy makers to bring about change?

Conclusion

In this chapter we provided an overview of the legislative and policy heritage that has shaped much professional practice with disabled people. From the Poor Law guardians through to hospital staff working in long-stay institutions, the continuous themes are of enforced options in daily living, inherent stigma attached to much service provision and even where philanthropy rather than categorical distaste underpinned provision, the result was often segregative services that perpetuated notions of difference and learned dependency.

In the following chapter we will look at the widening of choices for disabled people via community-based support and more recently to the growth of per-sonalised practices that in theory place disabled people in the 'driving seat'. The role of the Disabled Peoples' Movement and of some enlightened professional thinking has converged to assist in the development of more enabling service mentalities. Whilst this does not mean that disabled peoples' needs are met in full, it does provide the basis for greater independent living options.

Further reading

Barton, L. (2001) (ed.) *Disability Politics and the Struggle for Change*. London: David Fulton.

Borsay, A. (2005) *Disability and Social Policy in Britain since 1750: A History of Exclusion*. Basingstoke: Palgrave.

Roulstone, A. (2002) 'Disabling Pasts, Enabling Futures? How Does the Changing Nature of Capitalism Impact on the Disabled Worker and Jobseeker?', *Disability & Society*, 17(6): 627–42.

3

Community Care
and Beyond

Introduction

In this chapter we detail the policies of community care that resulted in deinsti-tutionalisation and focus particularly on the original policy intentions and the realities of putting these into practice. We ask in essence – has care in the community worked as a policy and do communities care for disabled citizens?

Here also we aim to introduce the reader to the policies that underpin con-temporary professional practice and which have shaped the ways in which disa-bled people exercise their choices and rights in modern Britain.

Community care legislation

The Griffiths Report (1988) represented a challenge to institutional living policies. Griffiths, a civil servant, surveyed the provision for disabled people in long-stay hospitals and concluded in the spirit of the earlier Mental Health Acts of 1959 and 1983 that community-based options would be cheaper and more humane. Griffiths laid out a blueprint for community care which was later embedded in the White Paper *Community Care in the Next Decade* (DoH, 1990) and underpinned the NHS and Community Care Act (NHSCCA; HM Government, 1990). The key tenets of the report and subsequent legislation and guidance were:

- The continued shift of the locus of care from institutions to the community
- That informal care would form a key plank of community support

- That a purchaser–provider split would see social service departments moving towards a brokerage role and a mix of private and voluntary providers would deliver community care for those who continued to need funded support that could not be provided by the family
- Social workers became care managers rather than direct providers
- Cost was a key driver in community care, hospital care being seen as inherently more expensive.

Griffiths' ideas were not universally popular. Indeed the report managed to galvanise criticism from those interested in maintaining some long-stay provision for disabled people and radical critics of hospital provision. The following quote from a psychogeriatrician summed up the mood of some medical staff working in psychiatry:

> Arguments for more radical changes such as the creation for the elderly of 'a single budget in an area ... by contributions from the NHS and local authorities ... determined ... by a formula agreed centrally ... (and) under the control of a single manager' are not persuasive. They seem to be based in current fashions: to make radical changes every few years, an overenthusiastic belief that 'management' has magical powers beyond those of the caring and curing professions and the hardly concealed wish to include all provisions within cash limited budgets. (*Bulletin of the Royal College of Psychiatrists*, 1989)

A reading of the responses from medical professionals suggests both genuine concern as to the fate of many people with florid mental health problems, but others point more towards simply protecting the status quo. The motivations of professionals were mixed, as were those of the statutory architects of community care policies. For example, cost savings were seen as equally important by civil servants and politicians pushing through the NHSCCA. As Jenny Morris, a disability rights author pointed out, much of the cost saving was made possible not by shifting funding from hospital to community, but by relying upon families to pick up the tab for caring:

> Although a lot of effort has gone into the development of services aimed at carers in recent years, carers are not primarily consumers of services. Rather they are providers of a service which saves considerable public expenditure and the aim of policy is therefore to enable and encourage carers to carry on such unpaid work. (Morris, 1993: 37)

Indeed in many ways, the substantive provision of community care services continued to come from a more paternalist age in which sometimes 'imagined communities' (Bornat et al., 1993) acted as the vanguard for the new community care. In policy terms, the NHS & Community Care Act was similar in its assumptions to the Chronically Sick and Disabled Persons Act (CSDPA) 1970 and the National Assistance Act (NAA) 1948 in assuming that those services that would continue to be offered by the state would be assessed, shaped and delivered on the state's terms and seemed to offer little real scope for the choices and rights that had been mooted some 10 years earlier by the burgeoning Disabled Peoples' Movement. In this way, the paternalist assumptions (Braye and Preston-Shoot, 1993) that preceded the Act were carried forward to new policy and practice developments. The assumptions of the 'helper–helped relationship' (Finkelstein, in Brechin et al., 1981) and professionalised support (Mcknight in Brechin et al., 1981) were that disabled people sought assistance from health and social care professionals because they could not cope and this was embedded into the foundation of the NHSCCA.

Deinstitutionalisation

Deinstitutionalisation was begun in the UK over 40 years ago. In its simplest terms, the policy aimed to close existing long-stay facilities for disabled people, particularly those with mental health problems and those with learning difficulties. As we have seen above, the policy that replaced institutional care became known as 'community care' and it is still with us today, although in a barely recognisable form.

From the outset, it was not clear whether the policy makers intended community care to mean 'care in the community' or 'care by the community', which are of course, very different in intention and practice. Critical commentators (Bornat et al., 1993) were quick to point to the failures of the policy – inadequate community support services and insufficient resources have dogged the policy from the outset to the time of writing. However, with hindsight, it is hardly surprising that these were encountered. Community care policy represented the most radical change to service provision since the last Poor Law. Turning around the juggernaut that represented institutionalised care would understandably take a long time, massive resources, new forms of professional service and personnel, as well as new relationships with disabled service users.

The question of whether communities do or do not 'care' for their disabled citizens, has never been adequately answered. Arguably, if communities had adequately cared for disabled people from the outset, there would have been no need to set up the huge institutions in the first place and the massive investment and disinvestment of resources, both physical and human, could have been avoided. If we consider the millions ploughed into the long-stay hospital programme, exposed so eloquently by Goffman (1961), that arguably did little to improve the patients' mental health and resulted in lifelong stigmatisation and which ultimately represented a failure in policy terms necessitating the innovation of an entirely new community form of provision, we see the scale of the issues facing both patients and professionals.

Deinstitutionalisation itself did not proceed smoothly. The attempts to set up group homes replacing the hospitals proceeded with what was seen as indecent haste by some communities, not all of whom relished the prospect of absorbing the ex-patients into their communities. Whilst much of this could be seen as 'not in my backyard' syndrome, the pace of change and the numbers of ex-patients concentrated into small areas, undoubtedly put pressure on the already stretched emerging community services. The official response to such outcries was always to slow the pace of closure, but not enough to totally reassure communities that such new forms of service provision and the required levels of support would be adequately resourced. To compound these issues, the resources of the communities in question were themselves becoming severely stretched.

Communities are radically different in 2011 than they were in 1990. Most women, who historically have given time to community and voluntary projects, are now in the paid labour force (admittedly mainly part-time). This represents a massive shift in the availability of unpaid informal care and has had profound repercussions on women's 'spare' time to donate to their communities, over and above caring for family members. Simultaneously, men's roles as husbands, partners and fathers have expanded, enabling more of them to participate in domestic and family activities, previously the domain of women. The labour market has itself changed drastically, with more flexibility but much more contract working and insecurity of job tenure. All of these changes in economic and social conditions have had an effect on the amounts of available voluntary labour.

Critics differ as to whether deinstitutionalisation can be counted a 'success' or not. In the mental health field, which was of course the largest in terms of institutionalising disabled people, it is impossible to refute that if the term simply meant closing institutions, then it was evidently very successful. Similarly, in relation to 'intellectual disabilities', Emerson (2005: 79) states that: 'In 1976 there were just over 51,000 recorded NHS long-stay hospital "beds" for people with intellectual disabilities in England. By April 2002 this number had decreased by 93% to 3,638'. The success or otherwise of the deinstitutionalisation policy, over and above bed closures, is difficult to judge, not least because the policy itself resulted in a fragmentation of service providers, many of whom collect data in non-comparable ways (Emerson, 2005) and the issue of translating 'beds' into 'places'. However, Emerson demonstrated that the diversification of service provision and providers that resulted, when amalgamated, in broadly similar numbers. There are 'winners' and 'losers' in this game it seems: 'Total provision by the Independent Sector has risen nearly 15-fold from 3,200 in 1976 to 50,477 in 2001. The majority of this provision is in group homes for four or more people' (Emerson, 2005: 82). This generates some interesting questions concerning the original intention of the deinstitutionalisation policy.

WHAT DO YOU THINK?

Was the intention of community care to merely close large public facilities but generate many thousands of new ones, run by the independent sector?

Was there any evidence to suggest that care in independent sector group homes was better and more like 'regular life' than in the public institutions?

Do you think community care should mean care by the community or merely in it?

At the time of the introduction of community care, debate raged concerning the final question above – can and should communities care for disabled citizens? We have seen above, that the question taps into the moral and citizenship rights of all members of communities.

Disabled people obviously have a right to be part of their communities. Sometimes disabled people have care needs that community members and informal carers may meet. The question of the introduction of community care however, posed a moral imperative on the community. If non-disabled people choose not to care for disabled people, is this morally wrong? As many commentators suggested at the time, the vast majority of disabled people are and have always been, in their communities, not in statutory or institutional care. The indignant voices of informal carers and their associations were heard to proclaim that the government and tax-payers of the UK benefitted from the informal care they provide. One notable headline stated that informal carers save the UK taxpayer £87bn annually in care costs (BBC, 2007).

So, let us be clear, the policy of community care was intended to target disabled people who were previously in institutions and who would afterwards live in the community. However, the controversy did not end there. Many voices were raised about the pace of change and the rate at which ex-patients were being 'decanted' into communities (see above). Further controversy surrounded the types of accommodation that was being used. Some hospitals developed small group homes, some of which were actually in the hospital grounds, rather than outside the boundaries in communities proper. Questions were raised about this dilution of the intention of the community care policy, particularly in situations where large hospital buildings were being sold off to pay for the development of these sites. Commentators began to wonder whether community care actually had a different mandate than that given to the public.

Every policy, however radical, eventually settles down and becomes the norm. Arguably, community care has taken longer than might have originally been thought by the policy makers of the day. The extent to which a policy is more different and radical to what precedes it has a direct bearing here, and community care certainly has proved to be both different and radical. However, there is no question that disabled people have the right to the same quality of life in the community as non-disabled people enjoy. Therefore, any role that institutions may play in disabled people's lives following the introduction of community care would have to be of their choosing and volition.

In a society that views 'care' as a marketable item, just like any other, the above developments have sounded the death knell for public mass institutionalisation of disabled people and private care providers have been watching the situation with interest. The situation is now that the vast majority of disabled people live in the community, but many who challenge community service providers, still face either institutional care or life in the community under a controlled regimen. This is particularly the case for people with learning difficulties who challenge services (Emerson 1990, 2001). Thus, we have a situation where the majority of people with physical, sensory and mild intellectual impairments live in the community, whilst people with multiple, complex impairments, particularly severe cognitive impairment or mental ill health are much more likely to still live in some form of care home, albeit most likely run by the independent sector, and most likely a small group home facility. Thus, 'care in the community' has developed progressively with parallel meanings. Disabled people with 'mild' impairments are likely to live in ordinary accommodation in their communities using domiciliary services. Disabled people with 'severe' impairments – or those considered a threat to themselves or others – are most likely still institutionalised, albeit in much less obvious accommodation.

Thus, the challenge for the future is how to develop personal assistance solutions for the 'severe' group that are as close as possible to those we see for the 'mild' group. These personal assistance solutions would need crucially to allow for user choice and control in previously unconsidered ways. The challenges that this enlightened framework poses cannot be underestimated but must be addressed.

Arguably, one of the greatest challenges is assisting disabled people who have been institutionalised to overcome the effects of this and take control of their lives once more. The issue of institutionalisation effects only began to be seriously addressed once the policy of community care was underway. To the astonishment of policy makers, the effects, whilst most severe for the incarcerated disabled people, also extended to the staff (Thompson et al., 2000). Once a person's liberty and choices are removed, they quickly become conditioned into acceptance of the status quo. Under community care, giving disabled people back these choices turned out to be a major undertaking. For some people, therapeutic help and training can be used, but others will want to use advocacy and representation services for reasons of intellectual capacity or communication.

Many such services have sprung up, largely in the third sector organisations. Mostly these rely upon voluntary input from community members who are prepared to develop a long-term relationship with a local disabled person with a view to protecting their best interests, in situations where this is difficult or impossible for them to do so alone.

WHAT DO YOU THINK?

What does the term 'institutionalised' mean to you?

The absence of a rights-based approach to disability in the Griffiths Report (1988) and the White Paper *Caring for People* (1989) and the continued refusal by the UK government to embrace a Civil Rights Bill for Disabled People (from 1982 onwards) meant that otherwise ambitious policy shifts lacked a civil rights foundation which could have countered the professional dominance of disabled people that had preceded the NHSCC Act 1990 (British Council of Disabled People (BCODP), 1987; Davis, 1998). The established professional cultural values of institutions continued to permeate localised provision of support to disabled people, whilst community care itself in policy terms can be seen to operate with mythical assumptions about 'community' and the nature of 'care' in the 21st century (Bornat et al., 1993). In truth care often fell to siblings or parents of disabled people (Morris, 1993) in conjunction with a range of professional inputs where a community care assessment has provided for a package of support.

Criticisms of social workers' changing roles tend to ignore the top-down policy imperatives that encouraged care management away from direct contact with disabled people. Additionally, approaches more sympathetic to professional workers and often grounded in a practice framework (Sapey and Hewitt, 1993) noted that despite the best efforts of some social workers, the resource environment and the policy shift to Social Service Departments purchasing care but not providing it led to yet further fragmentation of community care. The assumption that these policy changes were welcomed by social workers is arguably unfounded. On this point, Beresford and Harding in *A Challenge to Change* (1993) note the irony of simultaneous 'openings and closings' in social care practice: the opening up of social work and practitioner education to more enabling training, language and practice points at the very time social service departments were forced to impose tight budgetary constraints. The development of user-led, user-involvement and rights-based services seemed to be cancelled out by harsh budgetary and care management environments.

More positive developments towards greater self determination were evident in the Disability Living Allowance & Disability Working Allowance Act 1991 and the Disability Grants Act 1993 (Drake, 1999: 63). These were two key legislations that shifted the use of welfare payments into the hands of disabled people. Disability Living Allowance for those deemed eligible provided mobility and 'care' funding which was paid directly to individuals and no check was made as to how the allowances were spent. Disability Working Allowance aimed to make work pay for those disabled people able to get access to the labour market but who were on a low income. This top-up benefit is paid through the national insurance system and is in principle less stigmatising. The Disability Grants Act ushered in the Independent Living Fund (ILF) which also made money available to people with substantial impairments who needed significant packages of support. Of note, these benefits were paid directly to individuals with no professional intermediaries. The ILF was an early example of direct payments of care packages being used which in turn engendered more choice in care markets and flexibilities. The benefit was limited to those in the 'greatest need' (Lakey, 1994). The Disabled Facilities Grant (1993) provided grants for home improvements to allow disabled people to remain in their own home. The means testing of this benefit however has served to limit the benefits of lifetime homes to a small number of disabled people with the lowest incomes.

As is often the case in social policy and practice, as one door opens another seems to close. Legal changes in case law in the wake of the above legislations further reduced social workers' discretion in the provision of support. The keynote case Regina *v* Gloucestershire County Council in 1997 established that whilst social care assessments were covered by a statutory duty for those deemed eligible for assessment, the provision against assessments could take into account the budgetary position of a local authority. This for some seemed further evidence that community care policy was primarily budget-driven, despite its rhetoric (see Cooper, 2000). In legal terms, the historical dilution of duties owed to disabled people under the National Assistance Act 1948, the Chronically Sick and Disabled Persons Act 1970 and the Disabled Persons (Services, Consultation & Representation) Act 1986 into more discretionary use of these statutes has de facto seen duties morph into powers, or enabling legislation. The rise of case law during the 1980s and 1990s is testament to this less than enabling role of disability law and policy. The view held by many sceptics that ending hospital care and fostering community care would not of itself save money seems to hold some water given the push to reduce spending on new community care services and attendant policies.

The irony of the increased targeting and case-law-based rationing of community care is that it took place against the backdrop of an increased rhetoric of choice under the banner of consumerist cultures promulgated in the Thatcher and Major (Conservative Government) years of 1979–97. Indeed it is noteworthy that superficially at least this emphasis on choices converged (inadvertently) with the UK Disabled Peoples' Movement's emphasis on reduced state interventions and the need for greater choices and rights for disabled people

(Roulstone and Morgan, 2009). Notably, rights has remained a preserve of radical social model writers, whilst choice has been championed by both left and right of the political spectrum. It is important to acknowledge, however, that for the UK Disabled Peoples' Movement choices and rights remains a meaningless notion without adequate funding. The year 1993 saw the publication of a landmark book in disability studies, Swain et al.'s *Disabling Barriers, Enabling Environments*. A broadside against the medical model of disability and professional dependency, it emphasised that despite decades of apparent reforms in policy and practice, professionals continued to:

- Perpetuate 'learned dependency' (Swain)
- Ensure the continuance of professional-led services (Oliver, Finkelstein)
- Perpetuate a 'needs-led' culture based on 'expert' assessments (Stuart).

This book captured the continued challenge of effecting greater choices and rights for disabled people. There were changes taking place in the delivery of services at this time however. By the early 1990s many social work and some health work contexts were beginning to recognise the need to afford disabled people greater control over and influence on the services they received. Empowerment curricula and service user involvement initiatives proliferated by the mid-1990s. The reality, however, was that 'empowerment' and 'user involvement' were taken to mean very different things. At one extreme empowerment simply equated to a living skills curriculum which was formulated by professionals to aid basic day-to-day skills acquisition such as handling cutlery (Fenton and Hughes, 1993). Whilst these courses have their value, there was nothing inherently empowering about them. Some social care writers discussed empowerment as though it was possible to give power to service users without losing power (Parsloe and Stevenson, 1993). This 'positive sum game' approach is questionable. Other writers made clear that empowerment if it meant anything had to involve a handing over of power by professionals if disabled and older service users were to be empowered (Barnes, 1997; Jack, 1993). Dave Ward and Audrey Mullender (1993), two key social care writers of the time, noted a similar domestication of the idea of 'user involvement' over time. When reflecting on the handing over of power and 'affording' disabled people greater control, it is worth reflecting that such ideas were not new, nor had they made a significant difference to the nature of key services in social care and special education. The following Acts all contained representation clauses:

- 1970 Chronically Sick Disabled Persons Act
- 1981 Education Act
- 1986 Disabled Persons Services, Consultation and Representation Act
- 1989 Children Act (disability provisions)
- 1990 NHSCC Act.

However, it is important to acknowledge where collaborative working has been successful and also where disability organisations have begun to challenge current practice and support agendas. In addition to the growing number of Centres for Integrated or Independent Living established during the 1990s (Campbell and Oliver, 1996), the 'All Wales Strategy', as early as 1989, helped to institute the involvement of people with learning difficulties in the planning, management and review of learning difficulty services. The role of advocates was seen as important here in establishing and maintaining the strategy. The shift of thousands of people with learning difficulties into group or staffed homes during the 1980s reflected the views of key advocates of normalisation (Wolfensberger, 1972) and of advocates of adequately supported community living (King's Fund Centre, 1980). The embracing of supported employment projects by many UK local authorities has to be acknowledged as bringing disabled people closer to the non-disabled world (O'Bryan et al., 2000). There are winners and losers here in policy terms, with people with mental health problems, sensory impairments and physical impairments receiving less statutory attention in these approaches.

Another key development in the 1990s was the passing of the Disability Discrimination Act 1995 (DDA). Although disappointing those commentators who had been pushing for full and enforceable civil rights (Barnes, 1991), the Act was symbolic in providing for the first time a right to legal redress where a disabled person had been found to have been treated less favourably for a reason related to disability. As Barnes and Mercer later noted:

> Political campaigning has been an important factor in the government decision to introduce major legislation such as the 1995 Disability Discrimination Act and the 1996 Community Care (Direct Payments) Act. Despite their shortcomings these have enhanced both disabled peoples' claim to citizenship rights and their participation in disability related services. (Barnes and Mercer, 2007: 137)

The DDA 1995 took disability and policy beyond the centuries-old tradition of voluntarism that had held back rather than bolstered enabling policies and practices with disabled people. The development of a new Community Care (Direct Payments) Act (1996) was more than symbolic however, providing as it did the principle of being allocated directly the funds with which to buy in social support and to exercise independence from statutory service provision for the first time. Notions of professionally driven empowerment that simply referred to a greater say in paternalist services were challenged with very new models of service delivery where professionals became the facilitators of support.

The 1990s also saw the development of less dependency creating day service approaches with the Changing Days programme, which aimed to improve the quality of day-time opportunities for people with learning disabilities. The King's Fund Centre and the National Development Team (for people with learning difficulties) 'supported five development sites that offered alternatives to segregated day centres by opening up opportunities in employment, education, leisure and other social activities' (King's Fund and National Development Team, 1996). Person-centred planning underpinned the programme and ensured that service users' views were at the centre of decision making about their lives. Future service planning and delivery were more generally reviewed within the programme. The programme has reported some successes. The scope for generalising from the benefits of the programme remains an open question, although there is little doubt that more recent emphases on choices in day services have been shaped in part by the Changing Days programme. Another important development at this time was the White Paper *Modernising Social Services* (DoH, 1998). This heralded the beginning of wholesale modernisation in social care where choices and independence attached to all recipients of social care and welfare support. The key tenets of the policy were to:

- Foster and support independence
- Provide more consistency in social care provision
- Support user-centred services.

The White Paper fed into the Care Standards Act 2000 which ushered in both new operating principles in social care and also new regulatory and inspection bodies including the Commission for Social Care Inspection (CSCI) to ensure institutional and local authority care standards, the General Social Care Council and a Care Council for Wales to which all social workers should be registered, and the Social Care Institute for Excellence to advance the 'knowledge base' in social care. The Care Standards Act 2000 (S. 80) brought forward new protocols for protecting vulnerable children, many of whom were disabled, by more careful screening processes in social care employment. These protections were strengthened further in the 2005 Care Standards Amendment Order to absorb the findings of the Bichard Enquiry (2004) which reported on the child protection lessons from the Soham murders. The years 1999 and 2000 also saw the passing of the revised Children Act (1999), needing the establishment of a Disability Rights Commission (HM Government, 1999a) to support legal cases and provide education on reducing disability discrimination. The year 1998 witnessed the passing of the Human Rights Act and also the passage of the Special Education Needs and Disability Act (1998) which expanded the 1995 DDA to include anti-discrimination in compulsory educational settings. It did not however outlaw segregated schooling (Barton and Armstrong, 2007; CSIE, 2004).

The passage of the Human Rights Act although seen as offering more than it can deliver (Daw, 2003) does present new opportunities for children and adults with severe and enduring mental health problems who are liable to compulsory sectioning under the Mental Health Acts of 1959 and 1983. Although not clarified by sufficient case law, the right to freedom and liberty contained in Article 5 of the Human Rights Act conflicts with the ability of the professionals to use the compulsory detention sections of these Mental Health Acts to detain patients involuntarily. In the field of special education, 2001 saw the introduction of a revised Special Educational Needs (SEN) Code of Practice (DfES, 2001). This Code laid out the graduated support disabled children should receive in both supporting their needs in school and in transition planning from year 9 to connect with further education, training and employment. The Code champions the view that disabled children's potential for life-long learning and employability should be thoroughly supported.

Some specific measures are mentioned in the Code of Practice which acknowledges the often overlooked area of speech and language therapy support. The provision of appropriate support and liaison with speech and language therapists is viewed as central to supporting disabled children via 'School Action Plus' or for a small number with very high support needs via a Statement of Special Educational Needs (SEN). Linked to this theme of communication, the Community Services Equipment Guidance was produced in 2001. The guidance proposed the requirement for a lead officer for communication needs planning and Joint Action Planning (HSC 2001/008 LAC 2001/13). Still on the theme of disabled children, the Children Leaving Care Act 2000 and Leaving Care Personal Advisor service were put in place to aid children (some of whom are disabled) to obtain suitable advice on moving into adult opportunities.

Perhaps the most wide-ranging policy development into the new millennium was the *Valuing People* White Paper (DoH, 2001a). Although restricted to people with learning difficulties, it offered an image of how future services should respond to the needs of this group and helped establish Learning Disability Partnership Boards as a forum for involving people with learning difficulties in the planning and review of local services. The first five years of the new millennium witnessed a proliferation of consultation and involvement forums. For example, Disability Independent Advisory Groups (DIAGS) were introduced to respond to policy issues. It is currently too early to say how effective these forums have been in shaping policy and practice.

A key shift in the field of child policy came about in 2004 with the advent of the *Every Child Matters* (ECM) Green Paper (2004) and ECM framework. The Green Paper was prompted by the enquiry into the death of Victoria Climbié and requires greater joined-up working by statutory and voluntary sector professionals to provide responsive and seamless services for children. New Safeguarding Panels were set up to review practices and policies to protect 'vulnerable children'. A number of follow-on policy developments such as Every Child Matters: Next Steps (DfES, 2004a) have been introduced to implement the ECM framework. The policy has led the establishment of a Director of Children's Services in each locality and a Children's Commissioner in countries that have signed up to the

Framework. One very tangible result of ECM has been the growth of co-located services, where public health and social services work together from the same building to ensure joined-up working. The recent *Aiming Higher for Disabled Children* (HM Treasury and DCSF, 2007) further commits money to disabled and sick children's services with an emphasis on short breaks, transition planning, childcare funding and options, palliative care, individual budgets and parental participation. It is too early to judge the value of these recent changes. What can be said is that commitments to better tailor services to children's needs are not new (for example the DfES (2004) 5 Year Strategy and personalisation of children's services, which followed on the coat tails of Every Child Matters).

In adult services, the arrival of the Green Paper: *Independence, Wellbeing and Choice* in 2005 has been seen by some to mark a major shift in the government's approach to future adult social care (ODI, 2008). This Green Paper, alongside the White Paper *Our Health, Our Care, Our Say: A New Direction for Community Services* (DoH, 2006) and the guidance contained in *Fair Access to Care* (DoH, 2003a), all emphasise individual choices in preventive approaches to avoiding inappropriate care options, maintaining independence and support tailored to individual needs (DoH, 2005a). Most recently *Putting People First* (DoH, 2007a) and *Independence, Choice and Risk* (2007b) have added to the message that social care solutions should be personalised, that money should follow individual disabled people and foster the 'self management of risk' (DoH, 2007b). In tangible terms, greater choice making will be facilitated by both more supportive professional values and practice, and specifically through the greater use of Individual Budgets and Direct Payments. Similarly, the widespread consultation that fed into the 2005 White Paper *Our Health, Our Care, Our Say* (DoH, 2006) also emphasises the importance of choice, joined-up working, the widest use of community resource, health prevention, wellbeing strategies and more flexible and reflexive service delivery. In day-to-day terms, the modernisation agenda has arrived at a number of key self determination and personalised mechanisms best captured in Person Centred Planning (DoH, 2002) Direct Payments (Glasby and Littlechild, 2002; Woodin, 2006) and Individual Budgets (Ibsen Consortium, 2007).

The rise of direct payments and individual budgets over time has led some writers to use the term 'Self-directed Support' to sum up disabled peoples' greater control of their support package. This rapid shift towards self-direction has predictably led to diversity of response, with evidence pointing to a lottery of provision of direct payments and some professional ambivalence towards the implications of greater 'choice' (Henwood and Hudson, 2007; Sapey and Pearson, 2004) particularly in relation to those identified as 'vulnerable adults' (Glendinning et al., 2008). Evidence suggests that people with learning difficulties often require additional support in direct payment use via brokerage services, whilst some applicants are deemed ineligible as they do not meet basic eligibility thresholds (Williams and Holman in Leece and Bornat, 2006). Notably, Holman and Collins

(1997) made early observations that pre-existing provision such as Independent Living Schemes and Trusts, needed to be able to connect fully with new direct payment approaches to empower disabled people.

What the above literature displays is a broad agreement that direct payments and individualised choice are inherently welcome and suited to disabled peoples' lives. It is unclear however, how broader policy shifts emphasising the central role of user-led organisations (Office for Disability Issues, 2008), which in the guise of centres for independent or inclusive living have historically been rooted in collective philosophical roots (Driedger, 1989), can connect with the categorical shift towards individual choice-making. Writing about mental health day services Bates (2007) emphasises the way in which provision offers 'safe spaces' and an opportunity for both solidarity and sanctuary for service users from often inaccessible and disabling mainstream spaces and locations. This however is a far cry from the Disabled Peoples' Movement's construction of collective struggle.

Other developments since 2000 include the Disability Discrimination Amendment Act (2005) which places an active duty on all public sector organisations to promote the position of disabled people and to reduce risks of mistreatment thorough a Disability Action Plan that must be completed and reviewed in a three-year cycle. The *Improving Life Chances* report was also published in 2005. This was a major review of the economic and social position of disabled people which makes a range of policy recommendations for both disabled adult and children's services (Prime Minister's Strategy Unit, 2005). The report has led to a further publication, *Equality 2025*, which was formulated by the newly established Office for Disability Issues (ODI) to outline key policy goals that need to be reached by 2025 that emanate from the *Life Chances* report. The Office for Disability Issues is a cross-governmental organisation that helps coordinate policy across UK government. One key ODI activity has been the development of a review of Independent Living across England, Wales and Northern Ireland. The ODI has also been instrumental in pushing forward plans for user-led organisations as a model for local planning and delivery of joined-up adult services. The Options for Excellence initiative being progressed by the DoH (DoH and DfES, 2006) aims to maximise the participation of users and carers and professional partnership working.

Conclusion

In this chapter we have provided an overview of policy, practice and approaches to disabled people over the contemporary period. We can see how approaches have broadly aimed to shift from those of containment, categorisation and segregation, to integration to inclusion. The reality is somewhat more complex. There are still several thousand people with the most complex support needs in institutional contexts (2,500 in learning disability beds, and 25,000 in mental illness beds) (DoH, 2008a), a recent study pointed to the limited community options for those recently spinal injured (Aspire, 2007) whilst rates of hospitalisation remain high for types of mental illness and distress (Cabinet Office, 2005). However, this should not detract from a fairly momentous shift towards community based options and the growth of involvement of disabled people in service planning and review. There are still abiding issues as to the adequacy of funding (NCIL, 2006) particularly in adult social care, and concerns that the latest forms of personalisation may be achieved by forms of rationing (Roulstone and Morgan, 2009). Overall, however, it is a challenging and rewarding time to be working in partnership with disabled people. There remain major but not insuperable barriers to disabled peoples' independence and to joined-up professional working. In subsequent chapters we will be exploring the above policies and the practice implications in much more detail.

We have introduced the reader to the British Government's modernisation agenda and set the legislative context that forms the backdrop to the key social policies that have been introduced in relation to disabled people's service provision. These laws changed the face of social policy for disabled people and as such are critical to understanding the current state of play in regard to disabled people in the UK. Successive key social policies changed the material position of disabled people over time. An understanding of these social policies is critical for all practitioners involved with disabled people. We have also seen how key turning points such as the Direct Payments legislation enabled disabled people to change the relationship that exists between them and practitioners.

Further reading

Emerson, E. (2005) 'Models of Service Delivery', in G. Grant, P. Goward, M. Richardson and P. Ramcharan (eds) *Learning Disability: A Life Cycle Approach to Valuing People*. Buckingham: Open University Press.

Roulstone, A. and Morgan, H. (2009) 'Neo-Liberal Individualism or Self-Directed Support: Are We All Speaking the Same Language on Modernising Adult Social Care?', *Social Policy and Society*, 8(3): 333–45.

4

Pivotal Moments in the Development of Disability Policy

Introduction

In this chapter we examine pivotal moments in the development of disability policy and begin by examining the social model of disability which has been hugely influential in shaping disability policy. Here we focus particularly on how the social model has developed over time in response to criticism and debate within the Disabled Peoples' Movement and academic disability studies.

This is followed by a discussion of 'mainstreaming' – the policy of inclusion of all children – and we examine key controversies and critique of this policy. We ask: Does a broad brush policy work for every disabled person? How can diversity be accommodated within a mainstreaming policy? What are the key issues for Deaf people and people with learning disabilities concerning mainstreaming?

The social enterprise In Control is explored as an important development in the history of service to disabled citizens as it seeks to foster and protect individual control without market individualisation.

We then examine the interface of social care with paid employment following the Pathways Green Paper of 2003, focusing particularly on Working Futures.

An exploration of the development of Personalisation, Personal Budgets and Direct Payments follows which heralded an important sea change in provision of services. Here we also discuss the issues involved in balancing greater individual choice with resource equity for a broad client base.

The development of new sets of relationships between practitioners and disabled people implies new types of service, new philosophies and new understandings, so this is followed by a discussion of Advocacy, Facilitation and Empowerment and finally we discuss the implications of Equality 2025 and the growth of Centres for Inclusive Living.

The social model of disability

The social model of disability was the innovation of a collection of hugely influential disability activists, but is largely recognised as the seminal work of Michael Oliver. In his book, *The Politics of Disablement* (1990) Oliver importantly changed the generalised meaning of the term 'disability' to incorporate ideas of social oppression. Thus, 'disabled people' to Oliver are people who are disabled (excluded/oppressed) by the non-disabled majority. The social model of disability made a distinction between the medical or individual model of disability (in which disabled people are viewed as individuals largely subject to personal tragedy brought about by impairment) and the social model of disability, which recognises the common oppression of all disabled people.

Importantly, the social model of disability is a mandate for political and societal change which has inspired many of the new laws and policies detailed in this book. As such, it was of key interest to social workers, and remains an influential and guiding force almost 20 years later. Since then, there have been many attempts to update, remove and rename the key tenets of the social model of disability (see Shakespeare and Watson, 2001; Swain and French, 2000; Thomas, 2007). For the most part these have enriched the disability research community, developing the original social model into materialist (Oliver, Finkelstein), feminist (Thomas, Reeves, Sheldon) and postmodern (Shakespeare) versions.

One criticism levelled at the original social model was that it was too focused upon the perspectives of white males, possibly persons with mainly 'static' impairment (e.g. spinal injury/wheelchair user), these being characteristics of the innovator. There is some truth in this, and the critiques and debates have, for the most part, refined general understandings of disability oppression. Importantly, Thomas (2007: 135–7) criticised the original social model's lack of consideration for 'impairment effects' – full recognition, for example, of the pain and inconvenience caused by impairment. Today, explicitly recognising the critique from our European continental colleagues, the UK obsession with getting the social model of disability 'right' has largely dissipated, and it is mostly recognised by the disability research community that there are many social models, and many and various ways of being disabled by modern societal structures.

'Mainstreaming' controversies and critique

'Mainstreaming' (integrating disabled children into regular schools) was a controversial policy when introduced, and in many respects, remains so. The policy evolved partly as a roll-on from the de-institutionalisation agenda (i.e. segregation bad, integration good), and it is possible that ideological zeal carried the policy forward, the protagonists little realising that some groups of disabled children may be disadvantaged in the process.

The policy hit the Deaf community particularly hard. Prior to mainstreaming, the majority of deaf children were educated in segregated schools for the deaf – large institutions, mainly residential facilities, which educated children often from the age of two years (Lane, 2002). By the time the mainstream policy came about however, numbers in many of the larger institutions were dwindling and it was becoming increasingly difficult to keep the schools open. However, what the policy of mainstreaming threw up was the critical position that the Deaf schools had held in relation to the learning and proliferation of sign language, which was immediately perceived as under threat from mainstreaming policy.

The historical development of British Sign Language (BSL) is a large subject that cannot be explored here (see Harris, 1995a). Suffice it to say, that although attempts were made to eliminate BSL in educational settings through the 'oralism' methods (forcing Deaf children to use any residual hearing and attempt to speak) this fortunately never succeeded (Lane, 2002). Deaf children who were fortunate enough to have access to Deaf adults and who had learned sign language before arriving at the schools continued to use it covertly and to promulgate it to their less fortunate peers 'behind the bike sheds' (Harris, 1995b). In the UK, many Deaf adults regard the oralist policy as oppressive (Baker-Shenk and Kyle, 1990) and some view it as an explicit attempt to stamp out BSL use.

By the time of the development of mainstreaming as a policy, BSL was undergoing a mini-revival; the British Deaf Association was gaining currency for its claim that BSL should be recognised as Britain's fourth indigenous language and successive campaigns for captioning (subtitles) on television had made a considerable impression upon the broadcasting authorities. In short, BSL was becoming trendy.

Enter mainstreaming – foresighted and intuitive development or yet another attempt to stamp out BSL use? The problem was that, even with the official oralist policy, the old schools for the deaf, as recognised by the Deaf community, served as the fertile grounds for the learning and practice of BSL by young deaf community members. Splitting these groups of children up and sending them to 'hearing impairment units' comprised of only a few pupils, would in effect stamp out BSL use. A young deaf comedian explains this here:

I went to a primary school for the deaf, where we weren't allowed to use sign language. We were forced to speak, using hearing aids. What was the point of that? It makes me angry just thinking about it. When the teachers' backs were turned, we used to sign to each other.

I learned nothing at school. The teachers told me I was rubbish. I used to get very tense and stressed out. I was good at maths, but I struggled with English. Even now

I find writing difficult. I use a lot of 'text' speak and struggle with more complicated words. I'll often ask a translator to sign things back to me if there are long words or lots of jargon.

At 11, I went to a mainstream school with a deaf unit. School was OK, but I had no deaf friends living nearby. The hearing children used to tease me a lot. I felt very low and frightened.

Education failed me. I left school with CSEs in woodwork and history. I didn't have any friends. I felt damaged by the education system, angry that I was discouraged from using my own, natural language. I hadn't been taught British Sign Language (BSL) at all. I'd picked up most of it informally. (*Guardian*, 13 May 2008: http://www. grumpyoldeafies.com/bsl/)

The dilemma therefore that arose in relation to mainstreaming was this – is it always best to be mainstreamed, or if you have particular characteristics (BSL user) should you be excluded from the policy? Surely, the main goal of the policy was not to exclude or segregate anyone?

Children with learning difficulties and their parents faced similar dilemmas, not so much on the grounds of language promulgation, but more on integration-ist issues. Arguments were put forward that stated that the public habitually discriminate against those perceived as different, often through cruel and stigmatising practices. The dilemma faced by professionals and parents was that whilst children with learning difficulties could be suffering from lack of stimulation and opportunity in special schools, they might also be benefiting from a lack of bullying by non-disabled children.

Pre-mainstreaming, parents of learning disabled children were routinely denied the opportunity to consider mainstream education as an educational choice. After mainstreaming took hold, it at least meant that the parents had to receive a reason why their child could not be educated within a mainstream school. The dilemma for the parents became whether to insist on full access to mainstream education and take the risk that their child would suffer bullying or go for specialised provision that risks labelling, stigmatisation and possibly low educational expectations.

One authority (OFSTED, 2006) that compared specialist with mainstream education options for children with learning difficulties found little between them:' ... effective provision was distributed equally between mainstream and special schools when certain factors were securely in place. However, more good or outstanding provision existed in resourced mainstream schools' (OFSTED, 2006: 1)

As with so many other policies, mainstreaming had laudable intentions but a broad brush approach to any disability issue is rarely useful. As we have seen above, there was no right or wrong way to interpret the policy, and the issue of mainstreaming is a good example of how a blanket policy can have unintended and undesirable effects as well as good intentions.

WHAT DO YOU THINK?

Think about the policy of mainstreaming in relation to all disabled children.

Take one impairment type (e.g. learning difficulties) and make a list of all the pros and cons of mainstreaming.

Which factors are more persuasive and why?

Balancing greater individual choice with resource equity   ● ● ● ● ● ●

Throughout this chapter we have seen how the significant 'moments' have built one upon the other, pushing the direction of policy and practice further away from mass provision and giving rise to more user choice and control in the delivery of services. However, one of the fears often voiced by governments and policy makers concerns the balancing of individual choice with resource equity.

Resources for health and social care, like everything else in life, are limited. In the modern welfare state, the issue of resources, and their scarcity, is always topical and provides the meat for political debate at both national and local levels. It is fair to say that in the UK we have one of the most top-heavy health and social care sectors in the world, but one that is the envy of countless nations.

For example, the challenges that the modern NHS faces on a daily basis include how to continue to provide service that is 'free at the point of delivery'. Successive debates have centred around eligibility for service and issues such as 'health tourism' have featured strongly in them. At the same time, the public's view on how much should be provided to whom has been the focus of debate. Personal (social) care is now (since 1 July 2002) provided free in Scotland but not the rest of the UK. This interesting development is emblematic of the fact that given enough political will, it is possible to expand upon the original intentions of the welfare state and community care. However, intentions and principles aside, there were many commentators at the introduction of this policy who believed that the system would not be able to cope and that there would be a possibility of an exodus over the border of people wishing to avail themselves of free personal care. It is certainly true that the amount of people receiving free personal care continues to rise every year, but it is not clear whether this merely reflects a growing awareness of free service:

> Personal care is now free for individuals living at home. In 2005–06, local authorities estimated the cost of provision at £168 million. This benefited some 41,200 Scots, so that the cost of the average home-based free personal care package was around £4,000 per annum, or £77 a week. (http://www.scotland.gov.uk/Publications/2008/04/25105036/13)

There is little evidence that 'care tourism' is taking place so far. The system does appear however, to be stretched and in some areas of Scotland there are signs that waiting lists are being used. In the evaluation for the Scottish Government that took place between February 2006 and 2007, it was found that:

> ... around half of Scotland's local authorities reported having people waiting for assessments to be completed, mainly due to a lack of staff to meet the demand for assessments. No local authority reported that assessments are being delayed because of funding pressures on their budget for providing FPC [Free Personal Care]. (http://www.scotland.gov.uk/Publications/2007/02/27143919/1)

The Scottish experience of launching free personal care is enlightening. In many ways it demonstrates that given enough political will, it is possible to expand on the intentions of the original welfare state, but, given the difficulties that have been encountered to date, it is possible also to see that undertaking such an ambitious expansion and delivering on its promises could prove difficult in the prevailing harsh economic climate, at a time when most countries are retracting public service provision.

WHAT DO YOU THINK?

If government policy allows for individual choice to be exercised, where does this end?

Will the demands of individuals not cost more than the state can afford?

How can individual demands be balanced across the client base, so that the limited resources are used equitably?

The lessons of history and new demands in practice

Social work has changed considerably over the past 40 years. The publication of the Seebohm Report in 1968 heralded a new era for social work – and a watershed for social services. New social service departments were created and, crucially, there was a move away from specialisms towards generic services, provided by generic social workers. However, genericism came at a price, and the price was inevitably that it was impossible for social workers to be all things to all 'clients':

> Under the successive blows of an economic downturn, child death scandals – starting with Maria Colwell in 1973 – and the rise of Margaret Thatcher, the sparkling new departments were, as one influential commentator put it, quickly 'transformed from a first resort to the last ditch' ...

It is difficult now to imagine the wave of optimism that swept over social work in those early days. John Rea Price, who became social services director in the London Borough of Islington in 1973, remembers the 'huge idealism' among social workers ...

What now looks much more out of place is the generic style of social work that the new departments struggled to implement. Seebohm set his face firmly against dividing social care, either by client age group or discipline, arguing that it disrupted continuity of care to families and fragmented the profession in just the way that the separate children's and welfare departments that had existed until then had done. By contrast, the new service would be family-centred rather than 'symptom-centred'. Since the aim of departments was to 'meet all the social needs of the family or individual together and as a whole', the committee insisted these needs should be served as far as possible by a single social worker ...

Rea Price, whose own department had more than 3,000 staff, says: 'Probably the major failure of the Seebohm analysis was not to anticipate the scale of the huge departments that its recommendations were creating, and the scale of the administrative, financial and management issues they would present. There was also the excessive faith in the generic approach to social work, but the stream of child death inquiries, as well as the rapid extension of the understanding of child abuse, soon began to expose the weaknesses of the non-specialised approach. (http://www.communitycare.co.uk/Articles/2005/10/20/51331/knock-it-down-and-start-again.html)

There is an old saying that states that if you wait long enough, everything comes back into fashion, and you could be forgiven for thinking that this is one of them, especially in relation to the origins and intentions for social work as a profession. The 'grand experiment' of generic social work departments is now over for sure, a failure of over-bureaucratisation, flawed initial intentions that had an anti-specialism fixation and an unrealistic vision of the human capabilities of social workers:

Lord Laming's inquiry into the death of Victoria Climbié led to an overhaul of children's services in the form of the Every Child Matters green paper published in 2003, and the Children Act 2004. These documents outlined a programme of reform across councils which are still being implemented. The major change involved the dismantling of traditional social services and the merging of children's social care with education and some health services, to form a children's services department, and the merging of adults' social care with some community health services. (http://www.communitycare.co.uk/Articles/2008/07/04/104021/childrens-services.html posted 4 July 2008)

These root and branch reforms have led some commentators to ask whether they herald the demise of social work as a profession altogether, since it has been effectively subsumed by Education and Health, or whether 'social work' as a profession will continue, albeit in another form and with different masters.

There is no doubt that social work as a profession appears to have been sidelined by the disabled person's movement and found wanting in terms of political allegiance, despite rhetorical appearances. This is regrettable as possibly there was an opportunity around the start of the 1990s for social workers to become facilitators and enablers within the statutory system. Instead, successive policy changes have driven social workers further and further away from their clients, turning them into managers of paper systems and 'assessment' regimens. This way of practicing was always going to be anathema to the Disabled Peoples' Movement.

The social model of disability took a very deliberate stance on expert power, aligning this with professionals of all stripes. Social work was too slow off the mark to see this occurring. Despite the flag-waving of many local authorities that they have been applying social model principles, it is fair to say that this turned out to be too little too late.

However, every cloud has a silver lining. The traditional social services with their emphasis on professional assessment, their reliance upon expert power as a mandate for 'intervention' and their inherently paternalistic approach have been overtaken by the new wave of service modes described in this book, which are much more in line with the social model of disability and the wishes of disabled people. As such, traditional social work's demise is similar to that of the dinosaurs. The government has both tacitly and explicitly recognised that the traditional forms of social service were outmoded in heartily generating and endorsing the new wave policies such as Personalisation.

Positive practice

Developments post-2008 suggest that integration of key services formerly under the guise of social work and social care is taking place, with Education firmly in the driving seat on children's services and Health likewise for adults. Where does this leave services for disabled people?

For those who believe that traditional social work as performed in social services pre-2008 was not a force for good in disabled people's lives, there will be little regret at its demise. Amongst the disability movement, there were many critics who voiced the view that professionals were largely part of the problem, not part of a solution; that 'experts' of all types are to be distrusted and that paternalism is par for the course when dealing with professionals (Davis in Swain et al., 2004).

However, what is not clear was whether it was social workers and social work that was largely responsible for the latter view – or professionals in general. If the latter, the developments post-2008 do not offer much prospect of radical change. Historically, disabled people's relationship with the professionals in Health has been as ideologically fraught as that with social work, if not worse. Whilst some social workers at least attempted to incorporate the social model of disability into practice and services in some areas (Harris et al., 2005), there has traditionally never been much of an attempt from their colleagues in the Health service to do likewise. Also, disabled people for the most part, given the realities of living with impairment, do not have a choice about whether to interact with the Health service professionals.

Unfortunately, one of the consequences of working within such a large bureaucratic organisation such as the NHS is that the ideals of the organisation tend to bulldoze past innovations such as the social model of disability. To a nurse, for example, a person is just an individual patient, not part of community that is stigmatised, oppressed and treated differently to the majority. It remains to be seen, therefore, whether disabled people get a better deal from the new adult system dominated by Health, or not.

One fascinating question that arises, is whether or not it is possible for professionals to base their practice on the social model of disability. Historically, the social model that was born from a reaction against the failures of the prevailing status quo (i.e. poor statutory service provision) was clear about what is unacceptable, but not so clear on what would be acceptable. Oliver's attempts to write about how professionals should act in relation to disabled people in his first book, *Social Work with Disabled People* (Oliver, 1983) gave very few pointers to positive practice, and subsequent editions still suffer from the same problem.

One project that attempted to integrate the social model of disability principles into the work of social workers, occupational therapists, care managers and assistant staff in one local authority was called the Outcomes for Disabled Service Users Project (Harris et al. 2005). Although, policy makers, professional bodies and disabled service users had all called for a greater focus on the outcomes of social care practice, a degree of confusion and disagreement about the concept of outcomes and its application remained. *Modernising Social Services* (DoH, 1998) acknowledged the importance of establishing and maintaining an outcomes focus in social care service provision, but noted changes in service provision had concentrated largely upon structures and process rather than on outcomes (DoH, 1998: para. 2.2). Clarity about intended outcomes of social care has been identified as a key element of recording in care management, but one that is often absent: 'Inspectors often discover that workers are not clear why they are intervening in a situation and how their intervention will tackle the problems or improve the lives of those with whom they are involved' (SSI, 1999: para. 1.23).

User groups and disabled writers have seen a focus on user-defined outcomes as central within user-led approaches to assessment and the development of standards (Morris, 1997; Shaping our Lives et al., 2003; Turner, 2000; Vernon, 2002). Making the concept of outcomes useable and workable in professional practice was seen as a first step in gaining credibility for both the concept of outcomes and the approach of outcome-focused practice, paving the way for user-defined outcomes.

The Disabled Service Users Project (Harris et al., 2005) used methods involving retraining all professional staff to use a focus on outcomes, specifically designated as the outcomes or end results that the service user wishes to see resulting from contact with the professional. The project was implemented in one large social services department in England which employed professionals to work in inter-disciplinary teams with disabled people in the community. The professionals involved were the Disability Service Manager, Manager, Care Managers, Social Worker/Care Managers, Social Worker Sensory/Visual Impairment, Occupational Therapists and Community Care Workers. The whole service was involved in the project which ran for two years in total.

In order to ensure that the professionals focused on the disabled person's desired outcomes, and to ensure that professionals did not lapse into making expert judgements on behalf of service users, the assessment and review docu-mentation for the local authority were redesigned around the outcomes focus. This ensured that the process of identifying the outcome was driven by the client and recording it was undertaken by the professional. Importantly, the whole process was driven by the service user utilising the principles of the social model of disability (Foster et al., 2006a, 2006b; Harris et al., 2005).

The results of the project were revealing. Service users rapidly became adept at identifying and implementing their desired outcomes and professionals largely managed to use the new documentation to record them and work towards them. The main difficulties encountered were with one element of the staff (Occupational Therapists) and comprised a reluctance to move from narrowly-defined perceptions of their professional discipline-based skills. Only this profes-sion felt threatened by the prospect of service users being in the driving seat concerning the direction of the work.

It was notable, however, that the vast majority of the professionals quickly adapted to the outcomes framework. Although the length of time the project could run proved insufficient for the ambitious goals, it was evident that disabled service users benefited from this approach and that they did identify and achieve their own outcomes. There was also evidence that the vast majority of profes-sionals (with the exception of the Occupational Therapists) found the outcomes framework a useful way of working with disabled people.

The importance of this project in demonstrating that even within the con-finement of a traditional social services sct up, disabled people could exercise choice and control so long as professionals fully understood that their role changed from 'expert' to facilitator and assistant, cannot be understated. Although a long way from total control and choice, such as a service user would experience in using Direct Payments or Individual Budgets, the project was an important line in the sand, in terms of what could be achieved through service users and pro-fessionals working together to achieve common goals. The project was pioneer-ing in demonstrating what could be achieved collectively by disabled people and professionals providing the former steered the process and the latter acted as facilitators only.

An important element in self-determination, and one factor therefore in being able to get the outcome that you wish to see, is the force with which you can impress this upon service providers:

> … practitioners will treat disabled people and carers differently as competent informers on a disabled person's needs, depending not only on the values and ethos of their team type, but also on how assertive a disabled person is, and whether they are judged by the practitioner to be a competent judge of their own level of risk. (Rummery, 2002: 69)

Rummery (2002) is here acknowledging the dichotomies that practitioners face in working with a service user wishing to take control, or use an outcome-focused approach such as that outlined above.

There is little doubt that disabled people do wish to exert control over service types and 'solutions' identified. It is precisely because it has been traditionally so difficult to get service providers to listen to disabled people's wishes that the Outcomes programme was instigated. The following data from the project (Harris et al., 2005) demonstrated how service users' wishes can get steam-rollered out of the way in the rush to provide a solution:

> Interviewer: … the most important thing for you was to find equipment or whatever that fitted in with your family …
>
> Respondent: Yes with all them, you know … even if that wasn't the most ideal piece of equipment when I said all these things about how I was going and how terrible it was, they just came with a load of gear and said you should have all these things. Now a lot of them are not pretty and they are not practical in a house with children, you know, and I hadn't, it's a small house. We've got three children and they're all huge and it's not, you know, things like toilet seat raisers, they're awful. They do the job but they're ugly and just bits of things and everybody kept coming 'Well you should have this. Well we'll bring it, we can, I can take it away' and they wouldn't let me say no, you know, and they had brought all these things and took them all back …

As the text demonstrates, the issue of aesthetics runs deep with many disabled people. As one recent project found (Harris et al., 2009), disabled people value technology and equipment that assists them to live in the community and prevents unnecessary hospitalisation or residential care. However, they most specifically do not want home to look like hospital. The text illustrates a common issue in service provision. Time and resources having become so limited in recent years has put huge pressure on practitioners to rush to a service solution. However, in the example above, little account was taken of how the service user felt about their home being overtaken with masses of equipment and the effects that this would have on the whole family. The 'solution' received by this service user demonstrates the need for the outcomes approach. If the outcomes approach had been used, the service user would have been in control of the direction of the solution and on each point would not have agreed to installation of equipment that did not fit in with the family, house or lifestyle.

Advocacy, facilitation and empowerment

Post-Seebohm and pre-2008, a number of interesting means of assisting clients were developed in the social care field and these were occasionally borrowed by other professions, particularly counselling and third sector organisations. Amongst these, and arguably the most respectable, was advocacy – the art of putting a client's points forward to a person in power, with the aim of establishing a course of action in the client's best interests (in situations where the person is unable to do so for themselves).

Many organisations today exist purely to advocate for vulnerable people and often these have charitable status with trained volunteers acting as advocates, particularly for people with learning difficulties, non-speaking people, or people with mental health problems. Our point here is not to describe or delineate the work of such organisations in detail, but to discuss the innovation of advocacy as a pivotal moment in the relationship between disabled people and professionals.

There is little doubt that in terms of making an impact upon wellbeing and social life, advocacy services have played an important role in disabled people's lives and have enabled many disabled people to get their point across to people in power. The idea of advocacy services in the UK appears to have been imported from the US. One of the foremost proponents of advocacy in the UK has been MIND:

Advocacy is a process of supporting and enabling people to:

- express their views and concerns
- access information and services
- defend and promote their rights and responsibilities
- explore choices and options.

An advocate might help you access information you need, or go with you to meetings or interviews, as a supportive presence. In some cases, you might want your advocate to be more active. An advocate might write letters on your behalf, or speak for you in situations where you don't feel able to speak for yourself. Friends, family and mental health professionals can all be supportive and helpful, but this may be difficult for them if you are doing things they disagree with, even though it's what you want. Health and social services staff have a 'duty of care' to the people they work with, which means that they can't support you in doing things that they think will be bad for you. But an advocate is independent, and will represent your wishes without judging them or putting forward their own personal opinion. (http://www.mind.org.uk/Information/Booklets/Mind+guide+to/advocacy.htm)

Thus, advocates have the status of trusted support to many disabled people and these relationships generally develop from contact with a voluntary organisation (such as MIND). The fact that the service is provided on a voluntary basis has been an important factor in the movement's success. Most organisations that support disabled people to use advocates run training courses for the latter and this is an important issue in quality control.

Facilitation is a term that has complementary and overlapping intentions with advocacy. The main differences here are merely that whilst advocacy has become the driving force behind a movement, latterly adopted in UK social policy, facilitation has a rather more loose interpretation. Basically, any action that is taken to enable a service user to access a service could be called facilitation work. As we saw in the Outcomes project, professionals can also act as facilitators to other services.

Far more controversial since its inception in the early 1960s is the concept of empowerment. Put briefly, there are, and always have been, a number of key issues in both the principle of empowerment and its practice that have dogged it until the present day. The first issue is conceptual. Empowerment means to give a person who has little power, more power – in particular the power to determine and act in their own interests. Here we can see the overlap with advocacy. However, looking closely at the empowerment concept, it becomes clear why it is as difficult to act upon. If a person has little power, say they are structurally disadvantaged through impairment and poverty, how can the intervention of a well-meaning professional alter this state – other than by removing the source or cause of their oppression (not easy when this is the majority non-disabled society) or by removing the effects of impairment (again not easy) or by giving them a considerable sum of money (even harder)? Asking difficult questions such as these is important even though answers are not always readily apparent. One positive course of action, for example, could be to align with the Disabled Peoples' Movement and campaign for better material conditions for disabled people.

WHAT DO YOU THINK?

What does 'empowerment' mean to you?

What issues do you foresee in trying to 'empower' another person?

The second issue is more practical and concerns power relations. Say you are a social worker, or a third sector worker and you work with disabled homeless people on a day-to-day basis. How would you go about empowering service users? What means would you use to convince people who feel powerless within modern society that they are in fact powerful and can act as change agents for their own benefit? Now we see the critical differences between advocacy and empowerment. Whilst the aims and goals of advocacy are conceptually clear and practically possible, those of empowerment are fraught at every turn with myriad issues.

A third issue that arises concerns class. Although politicians have been trying (unsuccessfully) to convince the general public in recent years that there has been a flattening out of societal structures and social class no longer exists in modern UK society, in reality this does not ring true for many disabled people. In the heyday of social work immediately post-Seebohm there was an explicit recognition of social class, including power differentials, and how they had historically shaped the lives of people in poverty.

Some social workers saw themselves as agents of social change, assisting underprivileged people out of poverty (see Adams and Campling, 1998). Thus, the radical social work movement generated ideas as to how this could be done (Jones and Novak, 1999). However, there was an acknowledgement that the people who were being assisted ('clients') were of a lower social class than those doing the assisting (social workers and other professionals). This led some professionals to question the motivations of the assistants and the feasibility of the endeavour. How could listening to the problems of underprivileged people lift them into a different class? How could the motivation to empower clients overcome the entrenched nature of the social class system of the modern UK? Most importantly, how would any of this work change the realities of power differentials between social classes?

The implications of Equality 2025 and the growth of Centres for Inclusive Living

Equality 2025 was established in December 2006 following a recommendation by *Improving the Life Chances of Disabled People*. The network works towards the Government's vision that, by 2025, disabled people will enjoy the same opportunities and choices as non-disabled people, and be respected and included as equal members of society. (http://www.officefordisability.gov.uk/equality2025/docs/appointment-rowan-jade.pdf)

Equality 2025 is a group of disabled advisors to the Westminster Government on how to achieve disability equality. The implications of setting up Equality 2025 are clearly that the government considers that true equality between disabled and non-disabled people has not been realised in the UK, despite a plethora of social policies and good intentions.

Centres for Inclusive Living (originally the 'I' stood for 'Independent') have grown exponentially in the recent past. Originally born (like the social model of disability) from dismay at traditional professional service levels and a desire to improve disabled peoples' experiences of living in their communities, their remit has grown significantly, especially and latterly in relation to the direct provision of services through service level agreements.

Centres for Inclusive Living represent a key historical moment in the lives of disabled people in the UK. They now form a huge network of centres, offering a vast range of services and support. Importantly, the CILs have championed and supported the development of Direct Payments (see above), the system through which disabled people can be paid the equivalent of the cost of traditional social service provision, which they then use to fund their care costs. Arguably, the Direct Payments policy would be much less successful as a whole, had the CILs not taken up the work of providing support and advice to those disabled people who wished to start using them.

Conclusion

In this chapter we explored the social model of disability and the widespread influence that it has had upon the shaping of disability policy in the UK. We then discussed 'mainstreaming' which has polarised debate concerning best practice in relation to disabled children. On the one hand, the majority may be better off under mainstreaming, but, as we have seen, there are very complex issues in mainstreaming deaf children and children with learning difficulties.

We have also seen how the social enterprise In Control has set out to radically change the basis upon which service is provided to disabled people in the UK. The Pathways Green Paper of 2003, Personalisation, Personal Budgets and Direct Payments all herald an important sea change in provision of services. Importantly in future service provision, there must be a focus on balancing greater individual choice and control with resource equity.

Further reading

Harris, J., Foster, M., Jackson, K. and Morgan, H. (2005) *Outcomes for Disabled Service Users*, Social Policy Research Unit, University of York. Available at: http://www.york.ac.uk/inst/spru/pubs/pdf/service.pdf

OFSTED (2006) HMI 2535: 'Inclusion: Does It Matter Where Pupils Are Taught?', http://www.ofsted.gov.uk/Ofsted-home/Publications-and-research/Browse-all-by/Education/Inclusion/Special-educational-needs/Inclusion-does-it-matter-where-pupils-are-taught/(language)/eng-GB (accessed 4 August 2009)

Shaping our Lives et al. (2003) *From Outset to Outcome – What People Think of the Social Care Services They Use*. Shaping Our Lives, National User Network, Black User Group, Ethnic Disabled Group Emerged, Footprints, Waltham Forest Black Mental Health Service User Group and Service Users' Action Forum.

5

Independent Living, Choices and Rights

Introduction   ● ● ● ● ● ●

In this chapter we discuss enabling practice in the 21st century and key laws and policy guidance documents that underpin practice. This is followed by an examination of work and economic participation and followed by a discussion of Direct Payments and their key place within the new Personalisation agenda. We explore the values of independent living and discuss how these can be translated into enabling practice. Next come the key concepts of choice and control – both critical to positive practice.

Thereafter we turn to a discussion of Independence, Wellbeing and Choice and In Control before concluding by discussing the innovation of Individual Budgets.

Enabling practice in the 21st century   ● ● ● ● ● ●

In the preceding chapter we discussed the growing movement towards independence, choices and rights for disabled people (Barnes and Mercer, 2007). Challenges came from both disability organisations (Campbell and Oliver, 1996) and from enlightened professionals (Braye and Preston-Shoot, 1993; Thompson, 1993) and were underpinned by legislative shifts to human rights and anti-discrimination legislation (Lawson, 2008).

At the policy level, in adult services, the advent of key policy documents, for example *Independence Wellbeing and Choice* (DoH, 2005a), *Our Health, Our Care Our Say* (DoH, 2006), *Valuing People* (DoH, 2001a) and the *Life Chances* report

(Cabinet Office, 2005) all pointed to the need to account for disabled adults' voices and to tailor services to their individual needs. In the field of children's services the arrival of Every Child Matters (DfES, 2003), SENDA (HM Government, 2001) and most recently Achievement for All (DCSF, 2009) provide major policy levers with which to improve professional practice. Although disparate, these developments all emphasised disabled peoples' rights to humane, equitable and responsive services. They all transcend the idea that professionals know best for disabled people.

Many of these developments are ambitious and some commentators point to the challenge of implementation in traditional professionalised settings and resource-limited health, social care and education environments (Barton and Armstrong, 2007; Renshaw, 2008; Roulstone and Morgan, 2009). However, there is no doubt that these developments are a major step forward in providing professionals who work with disabled people with a new language and mode of operation.

The challenge for professionals is not to lose sight of the key values mentioned above and to work reflexively (Braye and Preston-Shoot, 1993) to ensure wherever possible that services are commissioned, designed and delivered in a way that does not go against the principles of choices and rights. Many aspects of good practice do not cost additional resource (Sapey and Hewitt in Oliver, 1993).

As there are many possible areas across which choices and rights are being implemented, we concentrate on the following as they seem key to disabled people (adults and children) gaining greater social opportunities, going beyond a narrow 'corrective' or 'therapeutic' notion of practice to connect professional interventions with disabled peoples' wider life chances (Cabinet Office, 2005; Oliver, 1990). This means there are some perhaps unexpected topics which the authors gauge to be increasingly important in the lives of disabled people. These are:

• Work options and economic wellbeing
• Personalisation and Self-Directed Support.

Working futures: work options and economic wellbeing for disabled people

The 2003 Regulations (Social Security Incapacity Benefit Work-Focused Interviews Amendment) introduced a mandatory Work-Focused Interview (WFI) regime for claimants of incapacity benefits, that is, people claiming Income Support on the grounds of incapacity and Severe Disablement Allowance. The regulations required these claimants to meet a departmental official to discuss the prospects of a return to work and to access help to make such a return more realistic as part of the Department's Pathways to Work pilot scheme. The 2003 Regulations introduced the regime for new claimants in seven pilot areas only but these were subsequently extended and rolled out across the country.

These changes formed a significant sea-change in the development of services to disabled people because they introduced for the first time, the necessity for claimants to engage with officials concerning their capacity to work. Arguably, the onus was upon proving that work was not a viable option and why – this was certainly how the introduction was perceived by many disabled peoples' groups. Up to this point, although receipt of benefits was always subject to a strict battery of forms and medical tests via a doctor, there was no onus upon the individual to prove that they could not work.

Although many disabled people wish to work or to have access to paid employment that is flexible and pertinent to their circumstances, this move was seen as more 'stick' than 'carrot'. An important feature of these regulations is that they do nothing to counteract the structural issues that lie at the heart of employment issues for the majority of disabled people – lack of flexibility from employers, prejudice and discrimination in the work place from employers and co-workers and inaccessible workplaces or environments.

Traditionally, professionals working with disabled people have made assumptions that to require support signals distance from mainstream economic opportunities (Finkelstein in Brechin et al., 1981; McKnight in Brechin et al., 1981). Indeed the combination of 'care' and mobility benefits and receipt of direct payments can result in inappropriate assumptions that they are not commensurate. In fact there are no rules limiting the combination of paid work with the receipt of these benefits in principle as they are based on assessments of care, support and mobility needs in isolation from paid work.

However, there remains a degree of confusion about this area (Roulstone and Barnes, 2005). For example, the Department for Work and Pensions who administer Disability Living Allowance (a key non-means-tested benefit to fund eligible mobility and care needs), continue to assume that starting or restarting paid work is evidence of a change in a person's 'condition' (DWP, 2009). There is little doubt however that in time the philosophy of choices and rights which underpins direct payments will trump more traditional and 'top down' benefit assumptions.

What are the wider drivers of this change? Although likely to impact the next generation of disabled young adults, the major policy shift to ensuring that every child matters, regardless of their physical, intellectual and social status, is a key milestone for disabled children. Young disabled peoples' economic wellbeing is a key theme within Every Child Matters (see below). Whilst there is undoubtedly a long road to travel in realising its ambitions, the framework provides the building blocks on which to build disabled peoples' economic self determination in an era in which paid work is increasingly the mark of citizenship (DfES, 2003; DWP, 2005).

Viewed from the 21st century, commentators could be forgiven for asking what all the fuss is about as they may know disabled people who have well remunerated jobs (Shah, 2006). It is important to remember, however, that disabled people have historically faced major barriers to paid work. Those with very obvious impairments were for many decades likely to be viewed as unemployable (Barnes, 1991; Walker, 1981) or capable only of undertaking sheltered work (Hyde, 1998; Thornton and Lunt, 1995). Attitudes have shifted somewhat towards seeing disabled people in principle as being work-able, especially where adjustments can be made to their working environment (Gooding, 1996; Lawson, 2008; Roulstone, 1998; Roulstone et al., 2003).

Every Child Matters and *Aiming Higher for Disabled Children* (DfES, 2003; HM Treasury and DCSF, 2007) make clear the importance of the economic wellbeing of all children and young people up to age 25. Whilst lacking detail as to how early interventions can support later economic benefits, the policies, in emphasising educational inclusion and the extended school concept which allows wider social skills development and early responses to health issues, directly support the future economic wellbeing of disabled people and hold the promise of diminishing the assumption that impairment equates to unemployability. Until recently there have been few pan-disability professional approaches to supporting disabled people into and back to work. Indeed programmes rather than explicit professional roles has been the dominant approach – one that has often categorised disabled people into unhelpful sub-groups.

Disability employment policy and practice has been rooted in an anti-dependency rhetoric from the 1980s that makes some disabled people less rather than more attracted to paid work (Warren in Roulstone and Barnes, 2005). The notion of 'work for those who can and support for those who cannot' (Blair, 1997) which captured the New Labour offensive against growing levels of Incapacity Benefit claimancy, may also have inadvertently confirmed the position of disabled people furthest from the labour market as unemployable as it has led to 'cherry picking' of those closest to the labour market (Roberts et al., 2004).

The picture at 'street level' is not quite as bleak as it might first appear. Firstly, social service departments and increasingly third sector providers are involved in a range of supported employment schemes for disabled people (O'Bryan et al., 2000). These vary from subsidy models (the UK tradition) through to open market (US model) supported employment where disabled people receive market wages and may be supported by statutory or third sector initiatives in the form of 'natural supports' and job coaches (Jones and Morgan, 2002) to assist disabled people to familiarise themselves with a job.

Social service departments have had a long history of providing or purchasing such arrangements into supported employment. It is fair to say, however, that inter-professional links between Jobcentre Plus, the principal government employment agency, and wider social and health care professionals has been limited. Remploy, the government funded sheltered employment body has had a role in providing sheltered employment for people with substantial impairments who can still 'output' above 30% productivity; however this role looks increasingly under threat given the shift to mainstreaming and notions of choices and rights for disabled people (for debates on the value of sheltered employment see Hyde, 1998).

Perhaps the most significant shift towards widening the professional support towards paid work came with the Green Paper of 2002 on Pathways to Work (DWP, 2002) and the resulting Welfare Reform Act. Here community psychiatric nurses, GP practice nurses, occupational therapists and physiotherapists were all seen to have a fuller role to play in aiding return to work – something that has traditionally been undertaken by general practitioners.

The exact detail of such a role was not spelt out fully in the Green Paper, however there is arguably a much fuller role for para-health and social care professionals in building confidence towards paid work and providing health and occupational boosts to disabled people. It is somewhat ironic that occupational therapy, for example, has been largely delivered in abstract from real paid work opportunities and at times seems more akin to the 'warehousing' approach to disability than facilitating pathways to paid work (Barnes, 1990).

Social workers at present (often due to their large caseloads) generally only support disabled people following a crisis intervention – accident, dramatic deterioration in health or onset of significant impairment. Traditionally, for those clients of working age, they may well drift away from contact once social support is put in place, and most social workers will not have considered the interface with paid or voluntary work except where they have clients in day services (often those with more substantial support needs).

Social workers, care workers, key workers and community nurses have, however, been more involved in helping connect people with learning difficulties and mental health problems with paid work as these are explicit features of Valuing People (DoH, 2001a) and the National Service Framework (NSF) for Mental Health. The latter makes clear the need for healthcare workers to go beyond the realm of healthcare in supporting people with enduring mental health problems in the 21st century noting that: 'Working partnerships with agencies which provide housing, training, employment and leisure services will be required to address the needs of some people with enduring mental health needs' (DoH, 1999a: 7).

However, the recent piloting of Individual Budgets (IBs) takes social care professionals, both frontline social workers and case managers, closer to the world of work. Individual Budgets aim to move beyond the historically fragmented nature of provision for disabled people where assessment would often take place in many different service settings with no attempt to pull together seamless packages of support (DoH, 2005a).

The funding streams in IBs include 'care' type support, for example money to fund PA support, but also: Access to Work; Disabled Facilities Grant monies;

Integrated Community Equipment Services; Supporting People and Independent Living Fund (ILF) streams. Glendinning et al.'s early appraisal (2008) suggests that IBs are cost effective, do begin to break down artificial funding and support boundaries and do add confidence and control for some disabled people. However, research by the Consortium points to challenges in merging Access to Work and ILF integration funding with other social care funding streams (Glendinning et al., 2008).

Whatever the initial setbacks, there are a number of practice points for professionals that emerge from the above growth in the profile of paid work in the lives of disabled people of working age. These are:

- Professionals should not assume a clear and fixed binary between disabled people who can and cannot undertake paid work.
- As disability is a fluid relationship, the scope for employment may change over time given appropriate rehabilitation, wider health, social care and Jobcentre Plus input.
- The role of voluntary work and civic volunteering as paths to paid work or as meaningful activities in their own right need to be accounted for in your professional signposting.
- Do not assume that other professional groups will always take the lead on employment as they may be less aware of someone's situation than you are. You may be able to initiate more specialist support however from Jobcentre Plus.
- Some disabled people will not be able to work even with major supports and may have complex and profound support needs. It is very important to avoid traditional 'warehousing' approaches and to fully engage with active choices – for example sensory stimulation, queuing systems and other choice-based day services.
- Work as closely as possible with local disability organisations, especially local user led organisations (ULOs) and their networks as they are a valuable service information resource for professionals and will likely play increasingly important roles in service advice and in guiding enabling practice.
- Ensure you are fully apprised of supported options and providers in your locality for disabled people who may need support getting and keeping paid work. Be aware of national bodies such as the Association for Supported Employment: http://www.afse.org.uk/index.html
- Social firms operate and are supported in some areas as non-profit businesses well suited to the needs of some disabled people. For further information on social firms in your area see: http://www.socialfirms.co.uk/

For those people with more significant impairments, a referral to a Disability Employment Advisor (DEA) is required. DEAs are specialist Jobcentre Plus staff who offer a wide range of support, advice and information to disabled people as follows:

- An employment assessment to identify what type of work or training suits you best
- A referral, where appropriate, to Work Preparation, an individually tailored programme designed to help some disabled people
- A referral, where appropriate, to a Pathways to Work personal adviser
- A referral, where appropriate, to a work programme for disabled people, like the Job Introduction Scheme, WORKSTEP or Access to Work

- A referral, if needed, to a Work Psychologist for a more detailed employment assessment to identify the best work or training for you
- A job-matching and referral service – the DEA can let you know about jobs that match your experience and skills
- Information on employers in your area who have adopted the 'two ticks' disability symbol.

(http://www.direct.gov.uk/en/DisabledPeople/Employmentsupport/LookingForWork/DG_4000324 [accessed 3 April 2009])

It is important to note that many disabled people never get to see a DEA and are seen by frontline Jobcentre Plus staff. As a professional, you need to assist disabled people to obtain the best advice on which level of support is required. Also note that Access to Work has been dubbed the least publicised form of employment for disabled people and has to date been used largely as a scheme to keep disabled people in jobs rather than aid their access to employment (Roulstone et al., 2003). There is a significant role for professionals here in raising awareness, especially as the money committed to the Access to Work scheme was raised significantly in 2009 (Peck, 2009).

This funding increase alongside a government-led marketing campaign will hopefully ensure the Access to Work scheme is better profiled to potential beneficiaries (Hansard, 27/01/09 Column WA 27). For those people with the greatest support needs who aspire to work, WORKSTEP provides a phased exit from sheltered work to the open market where possible (Thornton et al., 2004).

Recent developments around Individual Budgets (IBs) require professionals to monitor carefully the local context. Where IBs have been piloted there may be a rapid shift towards merged budgets and care managers will need to work with personal brokers, advocates, family or friends in sourcing these merged funding streams to ensure that wider agency buy-in is achieved. The permanent lead professional and their disciplinary base (social work, health, employment) are still to be established and need careful monitoring to afford the most seamless process possible in supporting disabled people into work, or in work preparation or training. IBs under the pilot schemes were led by social care organisations (Glendinning et al., 2008). The mix of available options is confusing to say the least, however the following text taken from a progressive local authority helps point up the options in use for employment support:

Kirklees Council Employment Support for Disabled People (excerpted)

Signposting to *New Deal* (employment information, advice and support)

Signposting to *Disability Employment Advisors* (usually for medium to high needs)

Signposting to *Remploy* a sheltered employment provider.

Signposting to *Pathways to Work* – a scheme for people on Incapacity Benefits who need advice and support in returning to work.

Signposting to *Work Preparation* – a 6–13 week course for disabled people closer to the labour market.

Signposting to *Workstep*, a form of supported working with full market wages for those who need greater support in the workplace.

Better Health at Work – a Kirklees initiative to promote better mental health by improved working practices. Can support both employer and employee.

Balance Work–Life – A self help group to reduce in-work stress

Volunteering Kirklees – this aids steps to paid employment by providing confidence through voluntary work experience

(http://www.kirklees.gov.uk/community/care-support/health/mentalhealth/pdf/7_employment.pdf)

Direct Payments and In Control: blazing a trail for personalised social care

Whilst *Valuing People* began to sketch out more personalised service futures for people with learning disabilities, a wider shift to choice-making was encapsulated in the Community Care (Direct Payments) Act 1996 (in Northern Ireland see Personal Social Services Direct Payments Order, 1996; in Scotland see Community Care Direct Payments Scotland Regulations 2003). The legislation (which was pan-impairment) and guidance carried strong affirmative messages that disabled people should, wherever possible, be able to use funding to purchase their own packages of support. The legislation initially applied to disabled people of working age with the mental capacity to use Direct Payments. This was subsequently extended to older people (DoH, 2000) and most recently to carers of disabled people (DoH, 2005a; HM Government, 2000). For the purposes of the guidance, adult carers of adults aged 18 and over are eligible to receive a carer service. The legislation also covers 16 and 17 year old disabled people, parent carers of disabled children aged 16 or 17 years old and young carers.

Direct payments are means-tested assessed funds given in lieu of commissioned services, and are designed to provide disabled people with the means to buy in support and have greater control of their lives whilst being less dependent upon professional decision-making in the quality and nature of social support. Since April 2001 direct payments have also been made available to carers, parents of disabled children and to 16- and 17-year-old service users. Availability has also been extended to people with short-term needs, like those recovering from an operation, and to Children Act services to help disabled parents with their disabled children's support requirements (HM Government, 2000).

Perhaps the most innovative aspect of direct payments is the shift of disabled recipients from service users to employers, a shift that fundamentally challenges notions of disabled peoples' economic and social dependency that is assumed in much legislation and practice to date (Prideaux et al., 2009). Disabled people will, in most instances, have to deal with employment obligations. This can be slightly daunting. Some local authorities, however, provide brokerage and advocacy support to help with direct payment employment issues. For example, see the work of Disability in Camden in providing a typical range of support (http://www.discnwl.org.uk/direct.htm accessed 13 April 2009). Similarly, Essex Coalition of Disabled People (ECDP) has established a Direct Payments Support Service (DPSS) which:

> ... works in partnership with Independent Living Advocacy Essex (ILA Essex), screening all requests for Direct Payments. The client is then contacted to discuss their support requirements, and if necessary referred to ILA, who are able to provide face to face support. The Direct Payment Support Service also provides support and information to family members, social workers and their colleagues. (http://www.ecdp.org.uk/dpss/ accessed 13 April 2009)

Since their inception, a number of organisations, particularly the Centres for Inclusive Living, have developed services supporting those disabled people who want to take up Direct Payments. These service types are now broad, from information and advice on managing employees (e.g. from SPAEN, Scottish Personal Assistants Employers Network) through to complete management of the payment for the recipient.

The most obvious and pertinent features of the Direct Payments innovation, such as funds being paid directly to the disabled person, freedom over how these funds were spent, flexibility to act as the employer of one's own personal assistants or delegate this to a trusted facility (e.g. Centre for Integrated Living) were taken forward into the Individual Budgets pilots, which were largely successful for younger disabled recipients, but not as successful with older people. Despite the fact that as an economic measure, the policy saves them little, the current government is fully converted to this modus operandi and plans to roll this out further, particularly into Health services. Thus, we can expect to see more such innovations that give back to disabled people control and choice over their personal assistance, social care and Health services. See the following statement from the Department of Health:

> Across government, the shared ambition is to put people first through a radical reform of public services. It will mean that people are able to live their own lives as they wish; confident that services are of high quality, are safe and promote their own individual needs for independence, well-being, and dignity.

> This holistic approach is set out in 'Putting people first: a shared vision and commitment to the transformation of adult social care', the ministerial concordat launched on 10 December 2007 ...

Personalisation, including a strategic shift towards early intervention and prevention, will be the cornerstone of public services. This means that every person who receives support, whether provided by statutory services or funded by themselves, will have choice and control over the shape of that support in all care settings.

The work on direct payments and individual budgets, alongside that of In Control, are crucial to delivering greater personalisation, choice and improved quality. They are not separate initiatives or fleeting experiments, but fundamental components of a future social care system. (http://webarchive.nationalarchives.gov.uk/+/www.dh.gov.uk/en/SocialCare/Socialcarereform/Personalisation/index.htm)

Personalisation and Self-Directed Support   ● ● ● ● ● ●

The idea that support for disabled people should be better tailored to their needs is not itself new and has its origins in earlier developments (see previous chapters). Key precursors to personalisation can be found in the *Valuing People* document (DoH, 2001a), a key document in both symbolic and practical terms for people with 'learning disabilities'. Although there have been a number of interpretations of just what personalisation and personalised services are taken to mean across health and social care services (Mead and Bower, 2000) Brewster and Ramcharan's (2005) work is helpful in pointing to the centrality of listening to disabled people, their choices and capacity to choose, now and over time. It is seen as important not to simply adopt a 'once and for all' snapshot approach to personal choices and rights as circumstances change, for example in family, living options, life-cycle, key transitions (e.g. education, training and employment).

Valuing People applied the principles of personalisation in the form of Person Centred Planning (PCP). Such plans were to be based on professionals' understanding of choices and the conditions of choice-making; for example ensuring that choices are not unfairly or unreasonably constrained by professional, financial, family or local factors which can, with support, be overcome to afford maximum options. Valuing People and PCP conceived of support and living options being available from specialist/non specialist, formal/informal, personal and professional resources and networks (DoH, 2001b). Here is a summary of the basic tenets of PCP:

- Choices should be reviewed regularly.
- Choices should be ambitious, but not unrealistic.
- Choices should be conceived as coming from diverse sources.
- Choices, if meaningful, need to be based on capacity.
- Choice where capacity is limited can be aided by advocacy and brokerage.
- Choice should be followed through to ensure envisaged outcomes.
- Choice should be extended to all including those with complex needs.

The issue of ensuring the outcomes of the choice-making process are achieved is important as there have been instances in the wake of Valuing People where choices have been expressed but were not seen through (see Roulstone and Morgan, 2009; see also Harris in Barnes and Mercer, 2004). Brewster and Ramcharan's very helpful article on person centred approaches points to the need to see PCP as a 'process' not an 'event' (in Grant et al., 2005: 498).

The need to include all disabled people including those with complex physical needs is very important, with recent evidence that to date this 'group' has not benefited as fully from Person Centred Planning. At a strategic management level, the statutory requirement for Health and Social Care authorities to jointly plan through a Joint Strategic Needs Assessment has also not been that effective for disabled people with complex needs that substantially straddle Primary Care Trust (PCT) and Council services (CSCI and Health Care Commission, 2009). This report noted: 'Councils and trusts also had underdeveloped strategies for commissioning services for this group, while only a minority of service users had a person-centred plan, and in many of these cases the plans were poor' (cited in *Community Care*, 19 March 2009).

Valuing People established Learning Disability Partnership Boards (LDPBs) to better coordinate the commissioning of such services and these should be the first point of call for Health and Social Care leads to connect with the aggregated status of disabled peoples' requirements.

The UK and Scottish Governments and the Association of Directors of Social Work (ADSW) all accept that work is still needed to make the delivery of personalised services a reality. For example, in his Ministerial Foreword to the recently published *Changing Lives*, Adam Ingram, Minister for Children and Early Years, said,

> I know that a great many people working in the social sector are already taking this approach … However, more remains to be done and this publication will help develop understanding of the challenge for people working in social work services at all levels to make the delivery of personalised services a reality. (Scottish Government, 2009: 9)

Personalisation as a new means of public service delivery, despite being a new policy, is not at all new as an idea. Arguably, the underlying principles of community care are to support personalisation and the policy has been in place for almost 20 years. However, what is different about the current thrust towards personalisation is the determination to embrace so many of the tenets of independent living that have been at the heart of the disability movement campaigns for so long.

These are exemplified in the policy document, *Putting People First* DoH (2007a) Personalisation Toolkit:

Key elements are:

- Maximising access to **universal services** such as general information and advice, housing, welfare rights, learning, employment, public health, self-care, health promotion. This includes offering evidence based preventative interventions to **promote independence**, providing some people with the additional information and support they may need to make their own choices and to make a positive contribution towards their health and wellbeing.
- **Early intervention** to avert crises, to restore people's choice and control over their situation when needs have arisen and to support them with the least interventionist response (e.g. through re-ablement, avoiding hospital admissions, timely discharge, support to carers, one off grants, extra-care housing, use of technologies).
- **Personalisation of services and supports for those people who require ongoing support**, whether as self-funders or if eligible for state assistance. The main approach to this is through the development of a system of self-directed support within which people are offered an upfront allocation of resources – a personal budget (or their own money) – using this flexibly to decide how to achieve their desired outcomes. In addition **person centred approaches** and **information and advocacy services** are used to ensure that people can gain choice and control whatever their circumstances or type of services used. When developing these strategies to transform their systems, councils are also focusing upon the **cost effectiveness and efficiencies** needed to achieve ongoing sustainability and improvement. In doing this, they are combining tactical and strategic approaches, which release resources which can be put to better use in the short term while designing in more significant medium term benefits. As well as the necessary system, process and practice changes required to transform local delivery, councils are also starting to focus upon key enabling strategies. These include **partnerships with community and User-led organisations, adapting commissioning (including market development), workforce development and strong connections with other key service areas, especially health and housing**.

(http://www.dhcarenetworks.org.uk/_library/Resources/Personalisation/ Personalisation_advice/An_Introduction_to_the_Personalisation_Toolkit.pdf)

The scale and ambition of the personalisation policy can be gauged from this excerpt. Noticeable are the emphases on choice and control, coupled with a strong strategic direction towards prevention, both in terms of unnecessary hospitalisation and 're-ablement' – supports put in place to prevent escalation of 'intervention'.

The focus on joint working with user-led organisations is very new, but the focus on joint working between social care and Health and other public departments is not. There have been many and varied attempts to cajole and then force joined up working of public organisations in the past, it has to be said, with limited success. Largely, these have failed in the past from 'bunker mentality' – a focus on the individual department and their budget at the expense of others in the partnership. It will therefore be interesting to see how the partnerships referred to above will be different. They certainly involve new and more partners which is a welcome development.

Independence, Wellbeing and Choice and beyond ● ● ● ● ● ●

Some of the most progressive personalised support schemes have come from disabled peoples' own ideas. Whilst the significance of Direct Payments cannot be overestimated, limited take-up has meant that only 5% of eligible people were in receipt of direct payments some 10 years after the Act was passed (Davey et al., 2006; also see Roulstone and Morgan, 2009). Limited take-up, views that independent living had not taken strong root in adult social care and the growing demographic cost implications of an ageing population have led to redoubled efforts to 'modernise' adult social care.

Two key policy documents have been built within these contexts – the Green Paper *Independence, Wellbeing and Choice* (DoH, 2005a) and the White Paper *Our Health, Our Care, Our Say* (DoH, 2006). These policy documents began to solidify the spirit of earlier changes in adult social care by fostering personalised choices and the requirement for professionals to connect their work whilst placing disabled people at the centre of the decision-making process on social support. The key proposals of relevance set out in the *Independence, Wellbeing and Choice* are:

- Wider use of direct payments and the piloting of individual budgets to stimulate the development of modern services delivered in the way people want
- Greater focus on preventative services to allow for early, targeted interventions
- A strong strategic and leadership role for local government, working in partnership with other agencies, particularly the NHS, to ensure a wide development of new and exciting models of service delivery and harnessing technology to deliver the right outcomes for adult social care.

(DoH, 2005a: 14)

Independence, Wellbeing and Choice (DoH, 2005a) also makes clear the importance of required outcomes of personalised social support in improving disabled peoples' health, quality of life and economic wellbeing, support for disabled people in making a positive contribution, to exercise choice and control, to be free from discrimination and harassment and to have personal dignity (DoH, 2005a: 10). In practice terms *Independence, Wellbeing and Choice* alongside the later iteration in *Our Health, Our Care, Our Say* requires professionals in Social Care, Health, Housing, Employment and training to work to identify a range of proactive approaches, from preventive strategies through to multi-disciplinary protocols for supporting people with more complex needs, for example in terms of options for the following: short-term respite; intermediate care; and lifetime homes.

At a strategic management level this involves joint planning (e.g. through Local Area Agreements) and budgetary protocols that put disabled people at the centre of the planning process. At the level of operational managers and frontline professional working there is a requirement to be fully apprised of support options in the statutory and third sectors and to think beyond 'care' where there are wider wellbeing issues which might include work or leisure options for disabled people of working age. It is important to be aware of good practice resources such as those produced or maintained by the Social Care Institute for Excellence (SCIE), the Care Services Improvement Partnership (CSIP), and Patient and Public Involvement Resource Centres. Where things do go wrong it is important to ensure that the newly formed Care Quality Commission is supported in recommending improvements to services in health and social care (http://www.cqc.org.uk/ accessed 13 April 2009).

Of course some of the above changes are mandated and the recent *Putting People First* (DoH, 2007a) initiative laid a duty on local authorities to 'significantly increase' the number of recipients of direct payments and personal budgets. Indeed personal budgets – that is, budgets which have at least some element of direct payment – are seen as the baseline from which local authorities should build and signal an end to previous models of support. The initiative claims the first co-produced policy on adult social care and makes great play of the need to jointly organise assessments in a way that supports seamless services across Health and Social Care.

This reflects the shifts in the Darzi Report towards greater seamlessness across these previously very separate services (DoH, 2008c). Indeed, in terms of assessment, the policy places an emphasis on greater use of self assessment. This may be seen as creating a tension with the cost saving aspect of the policy (DoH, 2007b: 1) and we need to see how these are squared at street level. Certainly there is much anecdotal evidence that currently self assessments are 'moderated' by professionals. We need to ensure that such moderation is motivated by absolute cost concerns as opposed to developing cultures of constraint which limit assessed support as custom and practice. This latter would clearly conflict with personalised support principles.

The future shape of social work is likely to be strongly influenced by the changing transactions at the heart of direct payments, which are likely to affirm social workers as brokers and advisors on forms of wider support. It is likely that social workers will have a diminished role in assessment of 'need' given the shift to self assessment in the recent document *Putting People First* (DoH, 2007a) and the Office for Disability Issues' (2008) review of independent living. *Putting People First* draws together a range of observations on the best way to take forward adult social care. Key priorities identified are excerpted below:

- To emphasise preventative measures to avoid illness or impairment, and a rapid return to best health
- To aim for co-location of frontline adult health and social care bodies to afford seamless packages of support
- The better management of long-term 'conditions'
- Improvements in intermediate care provision (half way settings between home and hospital)
- Better hospital discharge arrangements
- 'Universal' information, advice and advocacy
- Carer support
- Better public/patient involvement
- Greater emphasis on self assessment.

(DoH, 2007a: 3)

The last point on self-assessment is very significant, symbolically and practically and will arguably be central to the enabling character of future adult social support as it gets right to the heart of the power relationship between service user and professional in the assessment process. It remains questionable how the government and its departments can square self-assessment with its imperative to save money in modernising social care. A clue is in the following cautiously chosen language that makes self assessment less than categorical, whilst leaving it as an important and valued option noting an emphasis on: 'A common assessment process of individual social care needs with a greater emphasis on self-assessment. Social workers spending less time on assessment and more on support, brokerage and advocacy' (DoH, 2007a: 3).

In Control ● ● ● ● ● ●

In Control started work in 2003 to change the social care system in England. The old system did not put people in control of their own support or life. In Control designed a new system – Self-Directed Support. The Government now wants all local authorities to change their systems to Self-Directed Support. Today In Control Partnerships is a social enterprise – a charity and an independent company. It works in partnership with citizens and government, and with charities and commercial companies. In Control's mission is to help create a new welfare system in which everyone is in control of their lives as full citizens. (http://www.incontrol.org.uk/site/INCO/Templates/SectionHome.aspx?pageid=14&cc=GB)

In Control was set up in 2003 as a project of Mencap with the support of the Department of Health's Valuing People Support Team. By early 2008 more than three-quarters of local authorities in England were involved. Ten authorities were working towards using Self-Directed Support as the approach for everyone needing social care support. To describe this as a quiet revolution in the social care sector is mostly accurate. Currently, most schemes are still nascent and although the potential is enormous and exciting, few evaluations of effectiveness have yet taken place. Should Self-Directed Support be rolled out across the whole of the UK in the future, it is likely that the relationships between disabled people and social care service providers will be transformed in very positive ways, primarily because disabled people will at last have control of their own outcomes and inputs from public social care providers. The model assumes the disabled person chooses and controls their own support in a similar manner to the outcomes framework (Harris et al., 2005). This in itself is revolutionary and has been the single most desired outcome for disabled people since the inception of transitional social services in the 1970s. The significance of In Control as a defining moment in disabled people's motivation to shape and control service provision cannot be understated and future developments will be watched with great anticipation.

A key feature of Self-Directed Support is control. The individual is always in control of the level of support and financial resources. In the very few cases where the individual feels unable to undertake control, the nominated substitute should always be as close to the individual as possible.

Originally In Control focused upon people with learning difficulties. Co-production of social care solutions was a key feature of the In Control pilots. The umbrella term *self-directed support* has been adopted widely since 'In Control' and embraces direct payments, and personal budgets. Personal budgets are budgets where at least part of the social care funding can be allocated on a direct payments principle, but where the fullest use of direct payments may be inappropriate or simply too early for a disabled service user (Samuel, 2009). Whilst able to choose the source(s) of social support, recipients of personalised budgets are at liberty to let social services commission personalised support.

This then is a sort of half-way house between traditional and self-directed support. There is in essence nothing new substantively in the term self-directed support, but it neatly sums up a range of related developments in adult social support. There is evidence that In Control has increased the number of direct payment users by demonstrating its benefits to a wider group of disabled people.

Individual Budgets   ● ● ● ● ● ●

Individual Budgets (IBs) stem, from the observation that for disabled people with a range of complex needs, service assessment, commissioning and provision have long been fragmented and at times counter-intuitive. Individual Budgets, in being tailored to the specifics of disabled persons' needs and in shifting attention from inputs to self defined outcomes in social care, conforms well to the personalisation agenda (DoH, 2009a). Following recommendations in the Life Chances report on IBs, a pilot programme was instigated and (following the principles of joined-up working) has involved a cross-government initiative led by the Department of Health working closely with the Department for Work and Pensions, and communities and local government.

The initiative has to date been in pilot format, with the pilot being completed with 13 local authorities between 2005 and 2007. Individual budgets are different to direct payments or personal budgets in aiming to pull together diverse income and delivery streams to approximate as closely as possible to seamless support. The key objectives are set out below:

- Service users should play a greater role in the assessment of their needs.
- Individuals should know the level of resources available to them.
- The pilot projects should test opportunities for integrating resources from several different funding streams into a single IB.
- The multiple assessment processes and eligibility criteria should be simplified and integrated or aligned, although adult social care should be the gateway to an IB.
- In planning how to use an IB, individuals should be encouraged to identify the outcomes they wish to achieve and the ways in which they wish to achieve them.
- Support should be available to help individuals plan how to use their IBs. Additionally, brokerage support should provide individuals with information on the costs and availability of different service options.
- The pilot projects should experiment with different options for deploying IBs. As well as direct cash payments, other potential arrangements include care manager-managed 'virtual budgets'.

(Glendinning et al., 2008)

Individual budgets then go much further than say direct payments in aiming to give control, to personalise support, but principally to pull together previously very disparate funding sources, as highlighted in *Independence, Wellbeing and Choice*: 'However, high levels of bureaucracy, repetitive assessments and piecemeal approaches to meeting individual needs indicate that extending the scope of individual budgets to closely allied services would benefit the individual' (DoH, 2005a: 34).

Funding streams would (where appropriate) need to take into account employment based needs, via the Access to Work scheme (AtW), substantial support needs through the Independent Living Fund (ILF), Supporting People (SP) and the Disabled Facilities Grant (DFG) and Integrated Community Equipment Services (ICES). These funds require the cooperation of the government department responsible as follows:

- AtW and ILF (Department for Work and Pensions)
- SP and DFG (communities and local government)
- ICES (Department of Health and Social Care strands).

Fund use flexibility was from the outset encouraged, and unlike direct payments, IBs could be spent on a much wider palette of choices to include leisure and recreation options which, for example, aid movement beyond dependency-creating contexts such as day centres. Social care providers are identified as the best organisation to lead on IBs, an issue that may be contested by other funding providers. The Ibsen Consortium (2007) evaluation of Individual Budgets established that the principle of IBs was generally well received, with some successes in implementation.

There remain reported challenges in achieving seamless budgetary alignment, especially involving health care budgets, whilst staff and service user concerns remain in some areas around the risk or perception of losing out if IBs are implemented. A more robust set of eligibility criteria, resource allocation and charging approach is still required if the pilot scheme is to be rolled out. There are voices which suggest IBs may not be as widely disseminated and available as once envisaged (Samuel, 2009), however it might be predicted that merged budgets are likely to be a feature of certain if not all the income/service streams identified above.

The idea of personalisation has not gone away despite the challenges of applying its bold principles in practice. Indeed the Department of Health recently launched a *Personalisation Resource Toolkit* (DoH, 2008d). The toolkit has been formulated from insights on personalisation to date.

Alongside the toolkit and pushing further ahead with user-led ideas, a parallel development of user-led organisations in 13 UK local authority areas aims to provide opportunities for disabled people in Action and Learning Sites to work alongside local heads of adult social care in pushing the social care agenda forward. The efficacy and coherence of the toolkit and Action and Learning Sites will depend upon sufficient funding and success in building further department funding concordats and relations with disabled peoples' organisations.

Conclusion

In this chapter we examined enabling practice in the 21st century and the key laws and policy guidance documents that underpin practice. A key question is how professionals can play a positive role in disabled people's lives. This is a complex issue that requires a rethink of traditional notions of professionalism underpinned by 'expert power'. To become a positive practitioner, it is necessary to examine critically the relationship that underpins engagement and to refocus the professional role on facilitation.

We have seen how the values of independent living can be translated into enabling practice. Understanding disabled people's choice and control is critical to positive practice. The disparate laws and policy developments discussed in this chapter may form the bedrock for positive professional practice.

Further reading

Barton, L. and Armstrong, F. (2007) *Policy, Experience and Change: Cross Cultural Reflections on Inclusive Education.* Dordrecht: Springer.

Prideaux, S., Roulstone, A., Harris, J. and Barnes, C. (2009) 'Disabled People and Self-Directed Support Schemes: Reconceptualising Work and Welfare in the 21st Century', *Disability and Society*, 24(5): 557–69.

Roulstone, A. and Barnes, C. (2005) (eds) *Working Futures? Disabled People, Policy and Social Inclusion.* Bristol: Policy Press.

6

Life Course Issues

Introduction ● ● ● ● ● ●

The majority of this book is focused upon policy and provision of services to disabled people of working age. However, any discussion of these themes would be incomplete without inclusion of the issues that impinge upon people and services throughout the life course. In this chapter, therefore, we explore key policy documents relating to disabled children, in particular, *Every Child Matters* (DfES 2003), before concentrating upon 'Every Disabled Child Matters' – a key campaign by leading third sector organisations launched in response to the former policy. We then turn to further key issues in childhood: wheelchair services for disabled children; growing up disabled; developing an impairment in later childhood; and the 'transition' from children's to adult services and the implications and differences in terms of service provision.

The policy anomalies and contradictions in the provision of service to older disabled people, and, in particular, professionals' lack of adherence to a social model approach, are then discussed. Assistive and advanced technologies are found to be important within home-based living options. Finally we explore the family context, looking at informal carer's issues and asking how professionals should balance the rights of the disabled person with those of the carer.

Every Child Matters: towards seamless child services ● ● ● ● ● ●

Every Child Matters (born out of child protection issues in the wake of the Climbié Enquiry (Laming, 2003)), focuses on a wide range of thematic outcomes and is explicit about five outcomes applying to all children, as the title suggests (DfES, 2003). Every Child Matters is principally concerned with the enhanced position of children's lives and ensuring that services and procedures (in cases of safeguarding) are joined up seamlessly.

Policy and practice issues explicitly around disabled children also stem from previous critical reports on disabled children: the Audit Commission report, *Services for Disabled Children* (2003), established major weaknesses in services for disabled children. The study explored the experiences of 240 disabled children and their families who described their experiences of public services, and shared their ideas for service improvement. The study found a postcode lottery of service provision and that receiving services was often based on the amount of effort parents put into lobbying for services (as opposed to equitable allocation models).

Services often arrived after some delay and later than service standards prescribed. Despite there being some pockets of good practice, services were not clearly advertised, application procedures were overly complex and frustrating to access. Together these specific and the wider observations of children's welfare services added impetus to the Every Child Matters programme.

There are five key outcome strands as listed below. The strand 'Achieving economic wellbeing' clearly relates to both current economic and later life opportunities and if successful will aid disabled children's transition to mainstream economic opportunities with shared expectations and achievements. Clearly supporting the other outcomes is also important given the holistic principles underpinning the policy. The five themed outcomes are as follows:

1   Be healthy
2   Achieve economic wellbeing
3   Make a positive contribution
4   Enjoy and achieve
5   Stay safe

The ambitions of Every Child Matters have since been translated into more specific guidance for professionals working with disabled children given their greater degree of poverty and social exclusion. The *Aiming High for Disabled Children* document is the key example of the ambition to see less disabled children in poverty and clearer more barrier-free pathways to social and economic inclusion in adulthood (HM Treasury and DCSF, 2007; see also Cabinet Office, 2005). One of the key messages of the policy is that traditionally services had been provider-led, patchy and at times not 'fit for purpose'. *Aiming High* states that: 'Engagement of disabled children and young people in shaping services at a local level results in the provision of more appropriate services, and can help services work more efficiently and effectively, allowing for more flexible and tailored provision' (HM Treasury and DCSF, 2007: 9). The task of an enabling practitioner is therefore to identify and encourage the fullest child and parental involvement in Parents' Forums and other Local Involvement Networks (LINs) and in their absence to work with social work managers and wider local authority stakeholders to facilitate such groups.

Another key challenge set out in both *Every Child Matters* and *Aiming High* is the need for information sharing to maximise the fit between service provision and a child's needs. In the area of safeguarding, professionals and local Safeguarding Panels need to identify as early as possible any major risks to a disabled child. A key message here is that it is no longer sufficient for a professional to argue that they assumed others were aware of a person's needs. Recent press stories point to the continued need to ensure protection of the most vulnerable children from both domestic and institutional harm (Mencap, 2007).

Every Child Matters sits alongside related policy and practice developments. Standard 8 of the *National Service Framework for Children* (DoH, 2004a) focuses on multi-agency working between Education, Social Care and Health agencies in the early identification of illness or impairment and the need to link Health and Social Care assessments as fully as possible for children with learning difficulties. Early identification helps ensure swift and sure Health and Social Care 'interventions', whilst evidence suggests that later life 'intervention' is often more expensive and less effective, for example in late response to joint contractures in childhood cerebral palsy (Green-Hernandez et al., 2001). Practitioners also need to be careful however not to over-medicalise where issues relate more to disabling social barriers as opposed to impairment (French, 1994).

Every Child Matters and wider children's legislation (DfES, 2003; DoH, 2008e; HM Government, 2004) has led to the co-location of much previously separate Social Work and Education services and often also takes in public and Primary Health planning functions. Professionals working in Children's Services in the early 21st century can expect to work closely in both spatial and practice terms with cognate professionals. Indeed some predict that named professions in say nursing or social work will diminish as services are increasingly planned, purchased and monitored jointly. Such an approach should help reduce the previously fragmented agency structures which were particularly marked for disabled children.

The *National Service Framework for Children* (DoH, 2004a) builds on other initiatives such as the Early Support Programme, set up in 2002. This is a partnership between the government and the third sector to improve the quality and coordination of services for disabled children and their families. This acknowledges both the shift of Social Services to be a purchaser not a provider of social care and of the growing importance of the third sector in responding to social and health care support. Parents have been at the centre of the Early Support Programme since its inception, helping to make multi-agency working and improved service provision a reality. Professionals clearly have a role here in connecting disabled children, their parents and involvement forums.

Every Disabled Child Matters

Every Disabled Child Matters (EDCM) was a campaign by Contact a Family, the Council for Disabled Children (CDC), Mencap and the Special Educational Consortium (SEC). It was launched in response to the Every Child Matters policy document (EDCM, 2009).

The Children and Young Persons Act 2008 received Royal Assent on 13 November 2008 and introduced an important new duty on local authorities to provide short break services. The Act is the government's flagship new law to improve outcomes for children and young people who are looked after by the state, or who are at risk of needing to be looked after. This of course includes disabled children.

EDCM got two important amendments to the Act. The first created a new duty on local authorities to provide short break services – this was the first time the law had required local authorities specifically to provide breaks. The second amendment was a new duty to properly support disabled children and their families when children are placed away from home. These were considerable achievements. It is too early to assess relative improvements as a result, but they are major steps in the right direction.

The issue of the provision of services to disabled children and their parents is one that, according to commentators (Priestley, 2003), has received insufficient critical coverage. Specifically, the developmental approach to childhood with its assumptions of a period of high dependency gradually diminishing and culminating in adulthood, when uncritically applied to the situation of disabled children, leads to the view that a disabled childhood experience is somehow incomplete and stultified, being trapped within a dependency relationship for longer than 'normal'. It must be remembered here that this was also the norm for disabled adults until the challenges of the disability movements of the past 30 years and that paternalism and stigmatisation are issues that pervade adult service provision at the present date to a lesser but still very significant degree. It is unsurprising then that disabled children are still seen by legislators and policy makers as being in a dependent and open-ended relationship with services. The challenge of reversing rigid assumptions and stereotypes is ongoing.

Evidence from the Every Disabled Child Matters and the Council for Disabled Children (EDCM, 2009) suggests there are still issues that need to be addressed in the implementation of Every Child Matters and Aim High for Disabled Children. This might be expected given their relative newness and the financially straitened times in which they were implemented (Roulstone and Morgan, 2009). One major specific focus on children and disability was embodied in the Bercow report (DCSF, 2008) on the needs of children with speech, language and communication needs (SLCN). The report discovered that services were poorly distributed, access to services was very patchy and that SLCN were often overshadowed by other child health and disability issues. As John Bercow MP, the report's author, points out:

> For far too long, speech, language and communication have been elbowed aside by policy makers in favour of other aspects of the child development agenda. Today's Action Plan is a welcome recognition by Government that communication must be given a much higher priority, nationally and locally, in the development of children's services. (DCFS, 2008: 2)

The report and action plan that followed on SLCN (DoH, 2008b) provides for pathfinder schemes to ensure that services are more equitably and carefully delivered to meet children's communication needs. Greater money was committed to this area alongside measures to identify SLCN as early as possible, to adopt whole family approaches and to connect SLCN services with wider health and social care provision. Speech and Language therapists have a clear role in implementing the above changes, but will require wider policy support from the Children's Workforce Development Council and in practice terms, school-based special needs coordinators (SENCOs) and early years staff will require support in identifying children's requirements as early as possible in their experience of formal play and education (DCSF, 2008). Children's Centre health care and child development staff will also have a key role to play in identifying and supporting children with speech, language and communication challenges (DCSF, 2008; DoH, 2008b). National third sector charities such as the charity ICAN provide web-based support to childcare professionals in gaining more skills and confidence in working with and supporting children's communication (http://www.ican.org.uk/early%20talk.aspx accessed 3 April 2009).

Aiming High (2007) requires that the commissioning of disabled children's services needs to take full account of local population needs and expressed views on services. Social Service and Health (PCT) authorities need to ensure that disabled children's services are not 'provider-driven' and best meet the needs of children in the locality.

Appropriate services rely in part on the careful commissioning of Health and Social Care services for disabled children providing services as close to home as possible, which are least invasive, work to reduce the medicalisation and difference of disabled children and which advance the wider social inclusion of disabled children and thus aim to enhance their wider life chances (see Cabinet Office, 2005)

There are a number of reported benefits to multi-agency working which suggests that there are inherent benefits to joining up our practice with disabled children and their families. Research by Townsley et al. (2003) on multi-agency working with disabled children who have complex needs, established that the multi-agency approach had clear benefits for disabled children and their families: 'Multi-agency based working provided effective, focused support to families to enable them to manage their child's complex health needs' (cited in McInnes, 2007: 17).

Research also shows the level of benefits to families in having a 'key worker' in coordinating the myriad of service and funding streams for disabled children. Sloper found that families with disabled children who had a key worker to coordinate services reported improved quality of life, better relationships with services and quicker access to services (Sloper, 2004; see also Young et al., 2006).

The Early Support (ES) programme, itself the result of the guidance document *Together from the Start* (DoH and DfES, 2003) brings together a philosophy of early support with practice tips on how best to prepare disabled children for the challenges of later life. Outcomes of the ES programme are measured in terms of the level of engagement of families of disabled children (0–3) and babies, access to services and the impact of professionals in their interventions. There are clear implications for Children's Centre workers, SENCOs and wider children's and early years professionals in joining up these early assessments, interventions and measured outcomes. The importance of a congruence between strategic and frontline operational professional understandings cannot be overstated in the context of early years provision for disabled children (Young et al., 2006). The challenge is best captured in the context of a child with complex health needs, where:

- Responses need to be coordinated to ensure all needs are met and that prevention is emphasized
- There is a clear lead agency which does not dominate practice exchanges
- Information is relevant to a child's health and impairment profile without unduly medicalising a child and not overlooking socially created barriers
- A keyworker approach is fostered to coordinate support wherever possible
- Information and service pathways/contacts are made clear and are accessible to the family
- Computer systems are networked and compatible
- There is understanding of whether universal or targeted support approaches are best suited to a family and child's needs
- Service assessment processes and eligibility criteria are made very clear. Especially where needs cross professional boundaries, service and budgetary flexibilities are very important.

Disabled children's wheelchair services: some distance still to travel

One area that now has government backing and which has needed policy and practice attention is the position and experiences of disabled children who require wheelchairs to gain and maintain independence. A survey by Staincliffe (2003) surveyed 145 wheelchair service providers and discovered that only 46% of authorities provided referrals for under fives, whilst fewer authorities that did refer and provide offered indoor power chairs for the under fives. Eligibility processes were inconsistent for children of all ages surveyed. One UK Member of Parliament felt so exercised by the question of deficiencies in children's wheelchair services as to put down a Commons motion: 'The provision of customised wheelchairs and other mobility equipment for disabled children is crucial in allowing children to develop independent mobility skills, confidence and self-esteem' (http://www.epolitix.com accessed 13 March 2009). A report by the Care Services Improvement Partnership (CSIP) *Out and About* (2006) pulled together a dossier of evidence to highlight the need for more and better tailored wheelchair provision if the above social inclusion aims set out in *Every Child Matters* (DfES, 2003) are to be substantiated. However, successive reports over the last 20 years have consistently argued for modernisation and investment in wheelchair services without which they will not be able to meet the expectations of users (CSIP, 2006; see also Audit Commission, 2003).

Clearly, any lack of suitable equipment risks limiting a child's development and is likely to place needless stress on the family. On a more positive note, the leading provider of paediatric wheelchairs outside of the NHS, Whizz-Kidz, has welcomed the government's child health strategy – Healthy Lives, Brighter Futures – which commits an additional £340m in funding over a three-year period to disabled children and their families. The funding is being allocated to Primary Care Trusts (PCTs) throughout England, giving them an opportunity to pump much needed investment into reforming wheelchair services, community equipment services and more short breaks for disabled children (http://www.whizz-kidz.org.uk/).

Good practice in wheelchair provision can be aided at strategic management level by good and frequent working contact with provider organisations. A local concordat between commissioner and provider organisations is important, whilst children and their parents should be included in these deliberations. Good wheelchair service provision entails:

- Joined up working – ensuring that health and social care agencies are involved (where appropriate)
- Clear and shared knowledge of lead practitioner – OT, physiotherapist, social worker
- Where funds allow, do not assume that wheelchairs for the under fives are of no social or therapeutic value – there is an evidence base stating these benefits
- Try to account for school and home needs in supporting the selection of a chair – desk, table heights, etc.
- Do not assume that because an individual can self propel, that they have to – check for issues of fatigue and scope in a typical week; professionals must account for day-to-day use, not idealised use.

The above facts concerning children's services are likely to feature in longer term practice developments and the following represents a summary of the 'core' positive practice points in working with disabled children and their families:

- Early identification and intervention
- Information sharing
- Assessment should be in a local familiar context – Children's Centre or school
- Fullest engagement with Parents' Forums or Local Involvement Network
- Holistic vision of needs
- Ability to work with other co-located professionals
- Making clear the boundaries of reasonable expectation of carers and care assistants who are not clinically trained.

Transition from children's to adult services

Although theoretically it should not matter at what age an impairment develops to the provision of services, in practice it can mean that there is a different relationship with service providers. Depending upon the impairment type, service providers from Health, Social Services and Education can theoretically have been involved with the child from birth and be providing services to the family as a whole unit (Arksey et al., 2002). This is a somewhat different trajectory to contemplate than one in which a child has an accident and gains an impairment in teenage years.

Generally speaking, in situations where children are born with an impairment, the relationship that develops is between service providers and the *family* primarily. Arguably, in these situations, it is slightly easier to get service providers to take seriously support issues, such as carer stress and the requirement for breaks from caring, because the family situation has been continuously under the spotlight of service providers. Also, should the situation be relatively stable and unchanging, service providers have the opportunity to provide significant assistance to the family, primarily because of the length of time over which the relationship can be developed.

In situations where a child develops an impairment at a much later stage of childhood, say approaching teenage years, the relationship with service providers in children's services is generated within a much shorter time-scale and in a situation in which the child is more likely to be the central focus of the work. This can have advantages and disadvantages for both the child and their family.

'Transition' from children's services to adult has been acknowledged as made much more difficult than it should be because of the lack of 'joined-up services' or ineffective communication links between departments (see Chapter 4). In such situations of transition, what is required is phased joint-working between children's and adult services, clear communication and a central focus on the wishes of the disabled young person.

The transition from childhood to adulthood can be difficult for many young people owing to pressure to conform to stereotypes in the media of the 'body beautiful' and peer pressure. Issues of sexuality and sexual awareness strike all young people, although disabled young people may face additional pressures (see below).

WHAT DO YOU THINK?

Disabled children and young people often face stigmatisation and discrimination from both their non-disabled peers and the general public. As a positive practitioner, consider your role in assisting disabled children and young people to reach their desired outcomes.

Working with older disabled people

Disabled people in the UK over the age of 65 (retirement age) form half of the total disabled population:

> ... there are over 10 million disabled people in Britain, of whom 5 million are over state pension age and 800 000 are children.

> This estimate covers the number of people with a longstanding illness, disability or infirmity, and who have a significant difficulty with day-to-day activities. (http://www.odi.gov.uk/docs/res/factsheets/disability-prevalence.pdf)

TABLE 6.1   Disabled people in Great Britain (figures in millions)

	Adults	Children	All ages
2002/03	9.7	0.7	10.4
2003/04	9.5	0.7	10.1
2004/05	9.5	0.7	10.1
2005/06	10.1	0.7	10.8
2006/07	9.8	0.7	10.4
2007/08	9.8	0.8	10.6

Source: Data in this table is from Family Resources Survey (FRS) Disability prevalence estimates 2007/8 updated (http://www.officefordisability.gov.uk/docs/res/dd/Disability%20Definitions.pdf)

Population demography suggests more people will live beyond age 70 and more than half the UK population is now aged 50 plus (Government Actuary's Department, 2003). Young adults with impairments are living longer lives

(DoH, 2008b). Life expectancy for all adults has increased by 11 years between 1948 and 2008 (King's Fund, 2009).

The prevalence of impairment increases as people grow older (DoH, 2001b). More importantly, changing sensibilities that have been born out of the disabled peoples' and older peoples' movements have questioned the historic dependency and lack of choice of older people in determining their lives (Phillipson, 1998; Zarb and Oliver, 1993). The challenge of providing choice, dignity and comprehensive services for older disabled people cannot be overstated.

Although much policy attention has attached to disabled younger people and disabled children (Cabinet Office, 2005) the policy position of older disabled people has received much less attention. Relatedly, the literature and research on older people and rights has tended to address issues of accessible housing, extra living costs, transport and lifestyle without much recourse to disability (OECD, 1996; Phillipson, 1998). It is perhaps surprising that any social work books avoid the term disability when discussing older age and social care. For example Gorman (cited in Adams et al., 2009: 95–6) adopts the term 'frailty' to sum up the service needs of older people. This is arguably a distraction from the commonalities experienced by those who do define themselves as disabled in older age (see Zarb and Oliver, 1993). There are a small number of works in disability policy studies that include or focus upon the lives of older disabled people (Priestley 1999, 2000).

Professionals working with disabled people need to be aware of the relative lack of voice that some older disabled people experience. In an era of proposed public sector spending retraction there is a real need for practitioners to maintain the dignity and choices of an often neglected but very large population of disabled people.

The presence of older disabled people within the disabled population in these considerable numbers is rarely acknowledged in either the literature arising in disability studies or policy documents. However, curiously, disability 'disappears' in policy terms once the age of 65 is reached and this affects the structure of service provision also. Therefore, if one has an impairment from birth and is in contact with statutory service providers, one's 'disability' is recognised up to age 65, but not the day afterwards. Therefore, in statutory service and policy terms, there is no such person as an older disabled person.

Curiously also, this anomaly has gone unchallenged by the UK disability movement for the most part, with very few notable exceptions:

> There has been very limited debate about the usefulness of links between later life and disability studies ... The social model of disability makes crucial the separation of disability from impairment and shows that it is society that does the disabling. This is never so clear as in the case of housing policies for older people ... Older people suffer discrimination and have to submit to a medical model of later life if they receive health or social care services. (Oldman 2002: 791)

It is therefore reasonable to question why this situation has persisted for so long, and why there is not more recognition of this issue. In policy terms, the effect of the above anomaly is to invisibilise impairment within the older population. Effectively, this means that governments 'expect' older people to have impairments, so 'disability' is not notable. In service terms, and as a person experiencing the transition from 'adult services' to older people's services, the effects are often dramatic, with inferior provision levels and less qualified staff contact, post changeover (Zarb and Oliver, 1993). Another frequently noted experience in this transition is the move from a welfare rights perspective to a traditional welfare receipt perspective. 'Disability' magically becomes de-politicised post-65.

Why were older disabled people, and their situation, traditionally not recognised by the UK disability movement, not seen as an allied oppressed group and their burgeoning numbers not incorporated into the cause? There is no clear-cut answer to this issue. The original social model of disability as conceived by Michael Oliver in 1990, has subsequently been criticised for concentrating too acutely on the situation of white, middle-class, wheelchair users of working age at the expense of almost every other impairment and status. Thus we have seen challenges on the grounds of sex (Thomas, 1999); 'race' (Banton and Singh in Swain et al., 2004) and sexual orientation (Shakespeare et al., 1996) as well as the exploration of other different statuses, including the situation of Deaf people (Harris, 1995a). However, as detailed above, very few authors criticised the original social model on the grounds of age (cf. exceptionally Oldman, 2002), nor have commentators been concerned to explore the reasons for the traditional service cut-off point, the policy disjuncture or the experience of inferior service provision post-65.

Perhaps the most disappointing development in disability policy in the last 10 years has been the limited attention given to this issue in the *Improving Life Chances* document (Cabinet Office, 2005), with only 10 references in a 244-page report devoted to older disabled people. Where older age is mentioned it is in the context of expanding employment opportunities and is arguably part of a wider push to activate disabled people of working age and examine the boundaries of what we define as 'working age'. This is a major disappointment and further ghettoises the position of older disabled people.

One of the major issues facing older disabled people is the funding of adult social care which for older disabled people is more likely to include provision for residential and home care support. The Royal Commission on Long-Term Care: *With Respect to Old Age* (also known as the Sutherland report; RCLTC, 1999) was established to look, amongst other things, at the best options for funding long-term care in an ageing population. In practice, the report looked at the funding of care for all disabled adults in both domestic and residential contexts. The commission recommended free adult social care in England and Wales to end the anomaly where health care was provided free in nursing homes but social care remained mean-tested. Despite means testing's continued links with the more stigmatised elements of the English Poor Law, the government decided not to implement the report's recommendations in full. Free personal care is however currently available in Scotland for older disabled people at present, although 'hotel' costs have to be met by individuals entering care settings (Scottish Parliament, 2008).

In the main, social care is means-tested in England for domiciliary, residential and nursing home personal care unless the extent or specialist nature of nursing care makes nursing/personal care inseparable or where health care is the clear primary purpose of the care package. A key policy issue has attached to the requirement on disabled or sick older people to sell their own homes where means-testing establishes their 'ability to pay' (Hirsch, 2006). This has provoked energetic political debates as to the fairness of this form of policy. In practical terms, once a house is sold, options for moving back into the community are often lost (Hirsch, 2006). There has been evidence to date of health authorities attempting to close facilities or refuse free care where personal and health care are inextricably linked. The Coughlan and Grogan cases establish in law the need for health authorities and PCTs to take full account of the degree of nursing care in concluding funding contributions (see http://carelaw.co.uk/press/court_clarifies_right_to_free_nursing_care.htm).

To make matters more challenging, fully funded NHS care in this context goes under a number of confusable names: continuing NHS health care, continuing care or fully funded NHS care. Although initially reluctant to issue standardised guidance to health and local authorities, the Department of Health's recent publication, *The National Framework for NHS Continuing Healthcare and NHS-funded Nursing Care* (DoH, 2007c) has confirmed the value of the ruling in the Coughlan case that nursing care funding is appropriate except where it is:

a) Merely incidental or ancillary to the provision of the accommodation that an LA is under a duty to provide, pursuant to section 21 of the National Assistance Act 1948; and

b) Of a nature that an authority whose primary responsibility is to provide social services can be expected to provide.

(R v North and East Devon Health Authority, ex parte Coughlan [1999]; see DoH, 1999b)

An issue that arose in Coughlan was the sanctity of an established home, in this case a specialist unit. The shift towards 'age in place' policies is likely to place greater emphasis on being supported with substantial health and social care packages in the home. The sanctity of the home is also enshrined in European law.

Article 8(1) of the European Convention of Human Rights states that everyone has the right to respect for his/her home. It is reasonable to sum up the policy and practice approach to residential and nursing care into the 21st century as largely reserved for short-term respite, intermediate care on leaving hospital or where complex health and/or social care needs cannot be met at home, for example in instances of severe dementia.

One area that has proven challenging for health and social care joint working has been the question of discharge procedures for older disabled and sometimes frail older people. Because hospital discharge aims to bridge hospital and home, environments where health care and social care each tend to lead on, there is much evidence of the limits of joint working, poor communication between professionals and, most worryingly, service users and carers having to face less than ideal circumstances when a person is discharged. There are a number of reasons for rushed discharge, for example where older disabled people are seen as blocking beds for people deemed in greater (acute) clinical need. The nature of some personal care tasks are also seen, quite wrongly, as not the business of health care – another reason for overzealous discharge. Rushed discharge can be disempowering for service users and carers, whilst in clinical terms there is a heightened risk of readmission (Bauer et al., 2009). There has however, been some evidence of improvement in joint working and the Department of Health has produced a good practice checklist in *Discharge from Hospital* (DoH, 2003b).

Another issue that arises is where a disabled person wishes to go home but they are seen as too ill and/or frail to return home by medical and social care staff (Chadwick and Russell, 1989). The negotiation of discharge or continued hospitalisation has to be dealt with on the balance of all available evidence and take account of home and family circumstances. In some health and local author- ities, the *Putting People First* (DoH, 2007a) and *The Case for Change* (DoH, 2008a) agendas take in both supported and appropriate discharge and the identification of preventable hospitalisation. This makes sense as both are about personalised solutions and also aim to ensure reduced risks of hospitalisation.

It is estimated that 2.5 million older people aged over 65 in England have some difficulty with activities such as 'dressing, eating, washing and going to the toilet' (Forder cited in King's Fund, 2009: 2). The question of who pays for domiciliary support is an important one. Means testing for home-based social care remains firmly in place. The Sutherland report noted that domiciliary support can be broken down into personal care and assistance with meals (for example meals on wheels). Sutherland suggested that as personal care was not optional it should be funded, but that assistance in the form of meals on wheels should receive a means-tested contribution. This was not embraced by the government of the day and free personal care remains a major funding and human rights issue.

Under the 'Fair Access to Care' (DoH, 2003a) eligibility thresholds (low, mod- erate, substantial and critical), local authorities have the discretion to adopt a threshold beyond which social care is free. In some areas the threshold is pitched at moderate need and above, in others it is restricted to those assessed as having critical needs. Research by the Commission for Social Care Inspection established that in 2007/2008, 72% of local authorities were no longer funding low or moderate needs. People who do not meet established thresholds with savings above a set level (currently £23,000) have had to find the cost of social care themselves. This 'cliff-edge' effect was acknowledged in the recent Green Paper on adult social care: *Shaping the Future of Care Together* (DoH, 2009b). For important adaptations to disabled peoples' homes under the Disabled Facilities Grant disabled people have to contribute on the basis of a sliding scale which although less steep than for personal care does make some work prohibitively expensive for disabled people who live just above income support or jobseeker allowance benefits levels. This has led to what can best be described as a lottery of provision where service eligibility and response to older disabled peoples' needs depends on where you live as much as the level of your personal needs. This sits awkwardly with the Personalisation agenda discussed in the previous chapter, and it is hardly surprising that the take-up of direct payments and personal budgets by older disabled people remains low. The government is currently reviewing these guidelines and the wide interpretations of its domiciliary care policies (King's Fund, 2009).

Adult social care and older people: practice issues   ● ● ● ● ● ●

The above point to a number of practice challenges. The current devolved principles of adult social care are double edged. The lack of central prescription over the eligibility thresholds to be adopted affords discretion as to just which threshold to adopt in making funds available. For senior and strategic professionals the task is to translate the philosophy of choices and personalised health and social care need into practice which maximises the amount of money that goes into front-line support services. As a strategic or senior manager you are well placed to ensure that funds are used to maximise independence and choices. This is clearly not easy, but only local health and social care professionals know the local terrain on which to place the most enabling service patterns. For example, in order to avoid the pernicious 'pillar to post' practices of 'decanting' disabled older people from hospital or specialist unit on to social care, the Health Act 1999 (Section 31) and more recently the NHS Act 2006 (HM Government, 1999b, 2006) allow joint funding flexibilities and also flexibility as to the lead commissioning organisation. It is absolutely crucial that senior staff account fully for decisions as to who should be lead commissioners and the exact terms of any flexible funding and delivery arrangements which place the enabling impact of joint working on the lives of disabled people. (For guidance on wider considerations in joint commissioning see: http://www.jointreviews.gov.uk/money/partnerships/savedScreens/checklist.pdf)

In the field of good discharge practice, health and social care professionals should build a dialogue with an older disabled person and their carer at the earliest stage possible. Decisions as to a discharge of an older disabled or frail person between, say, a senior ward nurse and hospital social worker should take into account the perceptions and concerns of the patient and relatives and should assess the risks of discharging too early. Ongoing clinical needs ought to be considered as it is not unusual for carers to pick up the tab for quite stressful and complex procedures. These issues should be central to health and social care professionals' discharge planning.

At the frontline, as it were, occupational therapists assessing for outline eligibility for the Disabled Facilities Grant should work openly with housing departments and social service departments to join up working to effect the most transparent and fair interpretation of the grant guidance as possible. Where eligibility is established, for example in approving major building works, professionals should be entirely upfront about maximum allowances for works and the scope for discretionary additional monies from social service departments. They should also help make connections with staff responsible for aids and equipment which might afford the best use of adapted premises. Good policy and practice in hospital discharge back home should take into account: the need for a designated person responsible for discharge; that decisions are always made by a multi-disciplinary team where significant support and risk issues are at stake; that discharge should be discussed at admission and not be treated as an afterthought; that the Single Assessment Process (SAP) should take discharge into account; and that roles and responsibilities are clearly defined (DoH, 2004b: 2).

Home-based living options for older disabled people   ● ● ● ● ● ●

The development and thinking of the UK disabled peoples' movement since the 1980s in the United Kingdom has helped ensure that community-based independence is part of the rights agenda, whilst government policy has increasingly converged with the idea of community-based solutions. Whilst the exact motivation for embracing community options is debatable (see Roulstone and Morgan, 2009), a key plank of the independence agenda is the role of assistive technology in helping disabled people gain greater control over their social environment. The recent emphasis on ageing in ones' home, or 'age-in-place' to use official terminology, increases the emphasis on home and community support (Means, 2007). There are a number of issues of which practitioners need to be aware.

Firstly there is the need for appropriate housing or housing adaptations. The Disabled Facilities Grant, a key resource for disabled people ageing in their own home is mentioned above. It is conceivable however that a person may need to move to a more accessible house. The provision of 'wheelchair standard' housing is significant here. The lesser category of mobility standard is more likely to be achieved through a retro-fit (after a house is built and lived in) approach, using, say, the Disabled Facilities Grant. Wheelchair standard housing may be required where retro-fitting would be difficult or prohibitively expensive. (An example of a wheelchair standard planning document is available at: http://www.islington.gov.uk/Environment/planning/PlanningPolicy/AccessibleDesign/)

Local authority plans have to follow the broad British Standards (BS) guidelines set out in the Building Regulations (Part M) (Office of the Deputy Prime Minister, 2000). Professionals do not need to be an expert on the details of these regulations; an understanding of the importance of accessible housing and being able to aid a disabled person's decision as to whether to retro-fit a current house or to initiate a joint professional application for a wheelchair accessible house is important here. Social workers, occupational therapists and sometimes community nurses may need to start the process of looking at accessible housing options. Whichever approach is taken, the direction of travel in policy terms is to age in place in the community – that is likely to hold for many disabled and frail older people.

For people with profound and complex impairments, such as late stage dementia or where sustained health care is required, options are likely to include residential care, nursing care or specialist health unit. It is also important to note that intermediate care options are becoming increasingly important in treating the health needs of older disabled people in community units designed to avert needless entry to long-stay residential or hospital settings. These units also aim to reduce bed blocking or too rapid discharges of older disabled people and act as a half-way option between hospital and home environments (BGS, 2008).

One key factor in age-in-place approaches is the perceived importance of new assistive technologies in supporting older disabled persons' housing needs. There has been a tendency of late for academic and practice writers to equate enabling technology (Roulstone, 1998) with Telecare (remote operated health and safety monitors or alarms). This is only one small part of the required picture. Indeed 'technologies of independence' is perhaps a better way to understand the assistive technologies that can facilitate older disabled people to stay in their home environments (Tinker, 2009). How can such assistive technologies be defined? A good working definition is offered by the Royal Commission on Long-Term Care: '... an umbrella term for any device or system that allows an individual to perform a task they would otherwise be unable to do, or increase the ease and safety with which the task can be performed' (RCLTC, 1999: 1). A basic understanding of the types of technologies that can assist older disabled people and their support professionals is laid out below:

1 **Devices to aid mobility and physical access**, for example wheelchairs (manual and electric), sticks, canes, mobility frames, wet room accessible showers, shower stools, bath hoists, grab rails, ramped access.

2 **Devices to aid communication**, for example telephonic devices including phone amplification, large button phones and text type (minicom) phones for people with hearing impairments.

3 **Devices to enhance environmental control**, for example the development of smart homes (hard wired and portable devices). Smart homes provide disabled adults with remote control of, for example, doors, windows, curtains, heating, lighting. The cost of hardwiring a smart house from scratch is high. The more affordable option is to retrofit a home with specific Environmental Control System (ECS) functions, to allow, for example, remote door and curtain opening, tasks that require significant 'gross' motor movements. One low-cost option which makes control of electronic items easier is a 'Global' handset controller for electronic goods which controls several devices in one (television, stereo). These devices are cheap and available from high street electrical retailers.

4 **Devices to enhance personal safety**, these devices include 'off the peg' rechargeable mobile or wireless portable telephones which may help reduce isolation and provide flexible access to emergency services. Community or 'Social Alarms' are the latest application of telephony to home-based safety. It is estimated that there are 1.4 million social alarms installed in the UK (DoH, 2005b). These systems can be telephone or pager based and can be worn as a pendant device for use in health emergencies, most typically falls in the home. For more information see the Department of Health's very useful overview of telecare *Building Telecare in England* (DoH, 2005b).

Technologies, both 'old' and 'new' can offer huge potential in supporting lifetime homes and ageing in place with dignity. Professionals should familiarise themselves with the full range and potential of assistive technologies, including those provided in the mainstream market (Harris et al., 2009). Those with a direct responsibility to identify assistive technologies (OTs, hospital social workers, community nurses) should also ensure they are fully appraised of local Community Equipment Services, and the local Telecare Improvement Network if one is in place (see: http://www.dh.gov.uk/en/Healthcare/IntegratedCare/Changeagentteam/DH_4123755).

It is worth noting that currently Community Equipment Services are undergoing a major re-evaluation which seems wedded to increasing the role of private retailers in providing more flexible and more user-friendly products and services (DoH, 2009c). The efficacy of this move is yet to be tested fully, however it is not difficult to see Direct Payments and Individual Budgets embracing Community Equipment in time to allow disabled people greater direct relationships with providers in the private and third sector (voluntary and charitable) providers. The adequacy of funding of such equipment is likely to remain a challenge.

A few warnings have to be issued in promoting assistive technologies based on research to date. Practitioners will need to be aware of the wider social factors that shape access to and service users interest in assistive technologies, as Lansley (2001) notes:

> ... despite the promise of assistive technology, the design of packages of assistive technologies to suit the specific and expected future needs of individuals, their incorporation into the home and their effective use are not straightforward ... The cost of installation, issues of who should pay, the disruption caused ... For many moving from the theory of assistive technology ... to the realities in practice will not be easy. (Lansley, 2001: 440)

This mismatch is most likely for major property refits or new build approaches which incorporate environmental control systems; however it is also likely where, for example, hoists are being fitted to afford greater access to 'social bathing' options. Cowan (in RCLTC, 1999) points out the 'postcode lottery' associated with assistive device provision and the need to avoid raising expectations ahead of an appraisal of likely funded support. Joined-up funding and provision are key messages to come out of recent reports from the Audit Commission (2004) and the Royal College of Physicians (2004).

Practice points with assistive technologies

When considering the role and use of assistive technology, be aware of the following points that emerge from research on the enabling and disabling uses of assistive technology:

- Be aware of the technological options available from a wide range of providers in the statutory, private and third sectors.
- If you work in a statutory body, follow the legislative guidance where possible and explore joint funding and commissioning potential.
- Try to avoid over-technologising a given solution in providing assistive technology and aids to daily living. It is very easy to forget the current generational issues in technology adoption and fear of computerised technologies. Over time attitudes towards technology will no doubt change, but issues of dexterity and potentially stigmatising technologies will likely endure for some service users.
- Be culture and gender aware in the assessment or provision of assistive technologies. Some cultural dynamics may be seen not to fit with wider familial assumptions on caring and support.
- Try to produce assistive devices that provide the least restrictive environments whilst offering a good measure of support. The level of technologising of solutions should reflect the risk of not providing such assistance.
- There is evidence that some authorities are attempting to reduce community care budgets by being over-reliant on technological solutions such as personal alarms. Remember, these should not be seen be seen as replacements for human centred support and safety systems.

- Involve specialist equipment services where needs are complex, such as in exploring smart home or major environmental control options,
- Some disabled people will have a good idea of their assistive technology needs. Empowering practice must extent to technological support.
- Strategic managers in health and social care should look at the seamlessness of their work as it impinges on assistive technology use. Health service managers should not assume that all home-based technologies are only useful in a domestic context – portability into health care, day care and respite contexts may be important. Joint provision and commissioning is likely in some care package arrangements.

(See Roulstone, 2007 and Harris et al., 2009 for useful guides to assistive technologies for disabled adults.)

Whilst arguably some of these features still pervade provision for younger disabled people, it seems a fact that the social model of disability has not actually entered the language of older people's services. Whilst many of the worst features are exacerbated by the scarcity of resources and the difficult times currently being experienced during the 'credit crunch' (from 2009), other issues such as ageist attitudes and low expectations of service quality appear to be entrenched. However, these features can be changed and a positive practitioner would seek to ensure that their practice is modelled on social model principles and subjected to reflexivity and positive values in order to ensure the best outcomes for disabled people of all ages.

The family context: informal carers' issues; balancing the rights of disabled people with those of carers

In a system that individualises and labels disabled people as patients and clients, it is easy to forget that they have families and that the latter always have and probably always will, provide the bulk of informal care.

In disability studies there has always been a tension between acknowledging the input and value of informal care and the primacy of the rights of disabled people. Indeed, until fairly recently, you could be forgiven for thinking that carers were invisible in the disability studies literature. This tension and the roots of the social model of disability have left a legacy that is still there today, although to deny the input of disabled people's families, especially in the provision of informal care and the role carers play in keeping disabled people out of institutions, is clearly not tenable.

Whilst not wishing to suggest that the movement of disabled people and carers' organisations are at odds with each other, historically they have not been happy bed-fellows, despite the closeness of the shared agenda of oppression by the majority society. This has much to do with the politics of care, as propounded by early feminists. In particular, Finch (1983) made a memorable statement in an early article that suggested that the expansion of the residential care market was sensible in order that the people providing informal care (overwhelmingly females) should be spared such work. Things have moved on considerably since those times, for example, it is now possible to be in the disability movement and be a feminist without suffering a crisis of identity. The underlying tension in the issue has not gone away however, and the ease with which medics and para-medical professionals continue to talk and write about 'carer burden' is discomforting.

The tensions between the rights of disabled people to personal assistance and those of informal carers, particularly family members, are difficult to balance, especially for professionals. To some extent, this has become easier as successive legislation has given carers the right to an assessment of their own service requirements under the Carers and Disabled Children's Act (HM Government, 2000). Some local authorities have taken advantage of the legislation to provide innovative means of enabling informal carers to take a break from care. This is not straightforward however. Many carers such as those who care for people with long-term conditions (especially terminal conditions such as motor neurone disease) find it difficult to 'turn off' from their responsibilities and there are also issues of finding good quality 'replacement care' that can be relied upon (Harris et al., 2003b). Each user–carer partnership of course is different and the balancing of service requirements by professionals has to be judged on its own merits. For professionals, this is a skill that develops over time.

WHAT DO YOU THINK?

What are the key challenges to professional working in an era of personalisation and choices for disabled people?

What are the key professional qualities required to ensure the policies and practices above are supportive of disabled peoples' independence?

Conclusion

In this chapter we explored the policy Every Child Matters (DfES, 2003) before concentrating upon Every Disabled Child Matters – a key campaign by leading third sector organisations launched in response to the former policy. We then explored wheelchair services for disabled children, growing up disabled and developing an impairment in later childhood, 'transition' from children's to adult services and the implications and differences in terms of service provision.

We have examined the policy anomalies and contradictions in the provision of service to older disabled people and in particular, the lack of adherence to a social model approach. Assistive and advanced technologies have been discussed as important within home-based living options. Finally we explored the family context; informal carers' issues and asked how professionals should balance the rights of the disabled person with those of the carer.

Further reading   ● ● ● ● ● ●

DoH (2004a) *National Service Framework for Children*. London: Department of Health.

Harris, J., Arnott J., Hine N. and Kroll, T. (2009) *The Use, Role and Application of Advanced Technology in the Lives of Disabled People*. Final report to the Economic and Social Research Council, UK. Available at: http://www.idris.ac.uk/book/Advance%20Tec/Project%20 Report%20FINAL%20copy%20for%20website.doc

Mencap (2007) *Death by Indifference*. London: Mencap.

7

Valuing Diversity

Introduction

In this chapter we examine how to value diversity, and begin with the key issues relating to mental health, especially the community care legislation and the ensuing policy and practice.

This is followed by a discussion of learning disability, especially issues of difference and societal pressures. We then turn to the small literature on disability and ethnicity.

Next we examine sexuality and parenting and the issues that ensue for professionals. Finally we consider how the diversity of disabled people as a whole has, until recently, been outwith consideration in disability studies and some possible explanations.

Mental health

As we have seen, the UK is still in the grips of the revolution that community care started, having had some 20 years since the development of the NHS and Community Care Act (1990). This may seem a considerable period, but in policy and practice terms it is not, especially considering the nature of the root and branch reforms that community care instigated. Future generations will look back at the NHS & CC Act as a watershed in the production and delivery of care to service users with mental health problems which quite simply was inspired and inspirational as a piece of original legislation, but which required a complete turnaround in philosophy as well as a revolution in service provision. The work of turning around the 'juggernaut' of mass institutional provision and more pertinently, institutionalised thinking (i.e. that disabled people belong in institutional care) may take the same amount of time to show significant change.

Everything changed following the Act – the huge institutional buildings were no longer fit for purpose, staff were retrained in patient-centred practice, and the patients who were incarcerated were decanted into small units. The debates that ensued following these moves have concerned whether community care, although widely recognised as inspirational, was actually less or more expensive, effective and/or more practicable than the previous regimes of institutionalisation (Means et al., 2008). There has been no disputation, though, of the fact that community care is the only humane and sensible policy to follow.

One interesting debate that ensued (which was long running and still not resolved) concerned whether the policy of community care actually meant 'care in the community' or 'care by the community'. In particular, feminists pointed out that 'care by the community' in effect meant care provision by women family members (Finch and Groves, 1983). In attempting to find 'non-sexist alternatives' to community care, Finch notably suggested residential care solutions, which did not meet with agreement from disabled people (Morris, 1993). The debate, though, highlighted one important issue that has never been satisfactorily resolved, which is that the original policy makers failed (and continue to fail) to appreciate the human costs of providing replacement care within families (Mansell et al., 2007).

Arguably, the types of provision that were developed for service users with 'enduring mental health problems' demonstrated that the devil was in the detail when it came to care *in* the community. These developments were often quite different from the intentions of the original community care policy. In relation to service users with enduring mental health problems, however, the distinction is critical and is as relevant today as it was 20 years ago. Proponents of the care in the community interpretation could see nothing wrong with service provision modes that replicated the features of the old institutions (distance between patient and staff; lack of choice, group-think service provision) but in smaller units. Hence, in many situations, small group homes were merely built in hospital grounds and the same (institutionalised) staff ran them. Whilst there may have been some small benefit reaped by some ex-patients in being able to live out of hospital, these situations seem to make a mockery of the intentions of community care.

However, those who interpreted the policy as 'care by the community' believed that the real revolution was in how service users were treated after deinstitutionalisation – as individual citizens, capable of making their own decisions concerning their future care. This mode had seriously different implications for service provision than the former mode discussed. At the heart of this provision is respect for service users and this is something that has had to be gradually wrested from service providers, largely as a result of disabled peoples' own efforts and that of campaigning organisations. Care *by* the community also implies that the people in the 'receiving' communities have a role to play in accepting and assisting ex-patients to reintegrate into the community. It has to be said that this role was not readily accepted and was in some cases, rejected. There was a feeling that this aspect of the policy was rather naïve.

However, being out of institutions does not necessarily mean that service provision in the community is easily set up and produced, as this blog from a service user demonstrates:

17 October 2008 | 03:34 PM

My CPN decided that I needed help around the home and to access social groups. So, as she is also my care coordinator, she made a referral to Social Services.

This was last Christmas 2007! They came and carried out a financial assessment. Then they decided I didn't need one because I'm on section 117. So they said that I didn't have to pay. Did I get services? No, I waited and every time my CPN came it was the same old story: her boss didn't want to pay out of his budget, so I then got referred for direct payments. This was Easter, and back to the same department that said I pay nothing, for another financial assessment. Now it's June and still no services. July came and I rang the department to remind them I'm on a 117. They sent me a letter stating that I didn't have to pay for services except meals and transport, still no services. Then they tell me that they have sent my file to the voluntary agency that help with Direct Payments. No address or contact number so I can follow it up.

I just wait and the months go by without access to services. I don't know how long I'll have to wait to hear from the voluntary sector, maybe by Christmas I'll get an appointment to see them. Then there is all the hassle of setting up bank accounts and employing people, keeping receipts, balancing the books and interviewing carers. Maybe next financial year I'll finally get the services I'm entitled to. I'll let you know, watch this space.

I still can't decide for myself which services I need as my CPN has to make a referral for the kinds of things she thinks I need. I think that I need a weight management class and an exercise group or relaxation groups, but she says she doesn't think they have any and has only given me 3 hours a week with a carer for help in the home. Social groups haven't been mentioned. But every 2 weeks they make sure I get my Haldol injection and I can be recalled to hospital at any time, as if that's all that matters. What about my quality of life? (http://www.rethink.org/about_mental_illness/peoples_experiences/blogs/ebony/the_long_wait_for_se.html)

As this account demonstrates, gaining access to services can be a lengthy process and even establishing that services are required can be difficult. Considering that service users with mental health problems have a propensity to suffer disproportionately from stress, having to fight to demonstrate eligibility scarcely helps. Issues of quality of life raised by the above blog, are frequently left off the spectrum, particularly in an economic climate of scarcity. However, as dramatically highlighted, quality of life is extremely important and can make the difference between merely 'coping' at a practical level in the community and feeling that one's contribution to the community is both valid and validated. Mental health service users, as the blog demonstrates, are only too aware of the conflicting pressures on service providers to both 'care and control'. This is evidenced in the statement concerning medication, which is frequently a core issue.

As noted above, the community care policy has been dogged from the outset by the issue of scarcity and equity in resource provision. As the blog above showed, these issues are as live today as they were at the commencement of the community care policy.

WHAT DO YOU THINK?

Read the blog again – what are the key issues raised by this disabled person?

Make a list of the issues on one side of the paper. On the other side, write what you think would be a good response from a caring practitioner.

Learning disabled service users

Deinstitutionalisation policies detailed above similarly impacted learning disabled service users, who have a long history of segregation from their original communities. In addition to the struggle to establish and keep community care services on an individual basis, learning disabled service users have stigmatisation issues that attach to deinstitutionalised populations in common with mental health service users (Goffman, 1961).

Deinstitutionalisation had many consequences for people with learning difficulties, not all of which were fully appreciated at the original conception of the policy. For example, possibly the only (tenuous) 'benefit' of institutionalisation was isolation from oppression, unpleasantness and ridicule by the public. A key survey by Mencap (2007) found that:

- Eight out of ten (82%) children with a learning disability are bullied.
- Eight out of ten (79%) are scared to go out because they are frightened they might be bullied.
- Six out of ten (58%) children with a learning disability had been physically hurt by bullies.
- Five out of ten (53%) children who had experienced bullying said that they stayed away from the places where they have been bullied in the past.
- Six out of ten (56%) children said they cried because they were bullied, and three out of ten (33%) said they hid away in their room.

- Four out of ten (36%) children surveyed said that the bullying didn't stop when they told someone.
- Three out of ten (27%) children surveyed were bullied for three years or more.

(http://www.mencap.org.uk/news.asp?id=2355)

Bullying then, arises from the 'difference' between disabled and non-disabled people. It is always unacceptable in whatever form it takes. Positive practitioners have a role in educating non-disabled people they come into contact with to understand the extent of bullying that exists for disabled people, the forms it can take and its unacceptability in civilised society.

Immediately community care became a reality, what we now know as disability hate crime (Roulstone and Thomas, 2009) also became a reality, particularly for any service users with physical differences from non-disabled people. This has generated an industry targeted at removing the 'differences' – for example, different facial characteristics in children with Down's syndrome. This in turn has led to a debate concerning whether this move is desirable and whether, for example, corrective surgery leads to other problems for the disabled person in invisibilising impairment. The Down's Syndrome Association position on cosmetic surgery is as follows:

The Down's Syndrome Association is committed to supporting families and their children with Down's syndrome. We do question, however, why some parents need to choose cosmetic surgery for their children, with all the discomfort and risk that any form of surgery entails. Hiding a child's disability also sends out mixed messages, not only to wider society, but possibly to the child itself.

We fully support the rights of adults with Down's syndrome to choose plastic surgery, although it is regrettable that they feel the need to change their faces in an attempt to hide the visible aspects of Down's syndrome.

Society must learn to accept people with Down's syndrome for what they are. Public perceptions and understanding have improved in recent years but we clearly have some way to go while demand for this type of surgery remains. A vital part of our role is to educate the public, helping them to understand and accept the contribution of people with Down's syndrome. (http://www.downs-syndrome.org.uk/news-and-media/policy/statements/235-cosmetic-surgery.html)

WHAT DO YOU THINK?

Should cosmetic surgery be offered to people with visible differences arising from impairment (e.g. people with Down's syndrome)?

Make a list of the possible benefits and demerits that could apply. Which of these arguments do you find most persuasive and why?

Other issues to surface almost immediately following deinstitutionalisation concerned fertility and contraception issues, including the right to found a family, which presented service providers with considerable challenges to their value-systems. Within institutions the professionals found it relatively simple to police sexual contact between people with learning disabilities. Outside in the community this was virtually impossible, which forced service providers (particularly social workers), to address the issue of how to support learning disabled parents in the community. This was a steep learning curve for professionals of all stripes, particularly those who were prepared to argue that learning disabled parents should simply have their children removed (see Llewellen and McConnell in Grant et al., 2005: 441–67).

> There is a small but growing body of international research on parenting by people with learning difficulties. Reviews of this literature … show that these families often receive a raw deal from the statutory services characterised by an 'over zealous' approach to the assessment of risks … and an underinvestment in the kind of services and supports that might enable them to bring up their children. (Booth, 2000: 176–7)

Even today, this issue still inflames virulent debate between disabled parents, their families and professional groups charged with supporting them. There are no formulaic answers to this complicated issue and in policy terms, debates concern the conflicting rights of the disabled parent to found a family (enshrined in the Human Rights Act 2000) set against the duties of the local authority to protect the child, but also to protect the parents as 'vulnerable adults' (see DoH, 2001a; and also Grant et al., 2005). This is a considerable policy and practice minefield.

A further concern to learning disabled people has been the issue of community participation, especially the right to work and earn money in regular and unsheltered settings (Goodley and Nourouzi in Roulstone and Barnes, 2005: 219–32). This is a difficult issue to address in practice, mainly because the primary issue is one of general public attitudes and tolerance.

As with so many issues in disability studies, oppression by non-disabled people is the major issue, with the largest and most insidious issue in this being discriminatory attitudes. Whilst the Disability Movement and its allies have made huge inroads into this area, and the force of successive employment policies have contributed to fostering more positive employer attitudes in particular, there is undoubtedly still a long way to go with improving the attitude of non-disabled people towards disabled people. One of the most pertinent features of attitudinal oppression and discriminatory attitudes pertains to non-disabled people's lack of tolerance of difference. Such intolerance is difficult to fathom – in reality every person is different from every other.

In April 2009 it was announced that the last NHS long-stay hospital for people with learning disabilities had closed. However, the deadline set by the NHS of April 2010 to honour the promises in the *Valuing People Now* policy document (DoH, 2009d) which contains the key objective of all people with learning disabilities and their families having the chance to make an informed choice about where and with whom they live, is likely to be missed. The April 2010 deadline was specifically the date by which all NHS campuses would be closed. As we have seen above, deinstitutionalisation for many disabled people, particularly people with learning difficulties, meant only moving out of a large hospital into a smaller group unit on the same site. Thus, the struggle to give all people the choices and rights to live where and with whom they choose is still not a reality in the UK in 2010, despite 20 years since the inception of community care.

One of the major issues preventing all people with learning disabilities having their home of choice is apparently a lack of joined up working by professionals from Health and Social Care, along with housing departments, employment and training departments (*Learning Disability Today*, August 2009: 11). It is frustrating to see that despite successive policies and local exhortations, and numerous projects (including the Outcomes project outlined above) to work jointly in order to produce contextualised outcomes that disabled people want, professional boundaries, budgets and within-discipline protectionism issues still stymie the efforts of the more enlightened policy makers and practitioners.

With more exposure of disabled people on television, general community attitudes towards disabled people appear to have improved,[1] and with the advent of the first British Disability Discrimination Act (1995), community attitudes at last have a real chance of changing for the better, albeit within a process of slow perceptual change.

Gender and disability

Like many other issues discussed in this chapter, traditionally gender issues were rather overlooked at the commencement of disability studies as a discipline. We have seen in the previous chapter how the overlaps and confluence of gender issues and 'care' have exercised authors and commentators, especially in relation to resourcing of community care and the viability of institutional alternatives. Although men do form part of the carer population, the majority of informal care is provided by women:

---

[1]The Deaf community noticed a change in attitudes towards British Sign Language use (and users) following the campaigns by for example Terry Riley and colleagues to get more BSL-interpreted programmes, as well as achieve more subtitling (captioning) of TV terrestrial programmes (Ofcom, 2007).

Women were more likely to be carers than men, 18 per cent compared with 14 per cent. There were no gender differences in the proportion caring for someone in the same household but women were more likely than men to look after someone outside the household, 12 per cent compared with 9 per cent. (National Statistics: http://www.statistics.gov.uk/pdfdir/cib0602.pdf)

It is not clear whether this situation arose originally and persists as a result of disparity in wages within the labour market (for example, it may be more viable for a woman within a family to give up work to provide care than a man) or whether it has more to do with women's so-called natural affinity/empathy with caring work. In relation to the future of informal 'care', as Swain et al. (1993) pointed out:

That some people *will* wish to have their personal support needs met through informal relationships means that there will still be informal carers. A continuing feminist analysis is needed to point out why, in many cases, it will still be women who become carers, but it must also start to incorporate growing evidence about the involvement of men … (Swain et al., 1993: 254)

As the authors go on to discuss in relation to the work of Morris (1991): 'Dependence on a partner or family member is exploitative to *both* sides if it is necessary because of a lack of any alternative' (Swain et al., 1993: 254).

Within disability studies, one original focus was upon whether disabled women are a 'multiple minority group' (Deegan, 1981), that is, whether and how the two statuses overlap and in what circumstances. However, unravelling peoples' identities is rarely a fruitful way to proceed and this has proved to be a rather sterile discussion.

In more recent times, gender has been acknowledged as highly significant in relation to ageing:

… the relationship between ageing and impairment is highly gendered. Women are likely to live longer than men and spend a larger proportion of their ageing lives with impairment … In addition, women are likely to be relatively disadvantaged due to the gendered nature of disabling barriers – for example in housing, transport, widowhood and institutionalisation … (Priestley, 2003: 151)

Thus, in policy and practice terms, consideration needs to be given to the ways in which gender and disability intersect across the life course and to address the disabling barriers that are produced at various points. One such point is when seeking employment: 'There is for example consistent evidence that disabled women … experience difficulties not simply because of the perception of bodily indifference, but as a social group who have historically been excluded from much public and paid work activity' (Roulstone, 1998: 32). Therefore, we can appreciate that societal disabling barriers have left a legacy which it will take time to dispel. Disabled women experience confounding oppressions over the life course, in various arenas.

Ethnicity and disability

Ethnicity and disability was traditionally not considered as presenting any separate issues of status or identity until the advent of postmodern thinking. This was evidenced by the almost complete lack of writing on this issue. A seminal text by Ossie Stuart in 1992 set out the parameters of difference in experience of services and general cultural differences and considerations. Stuart (1992) asked whether the concept of 'double oppression' was an appropriate starting point for considering ethnicity and disability, but found that the idea of 'simultaneous oppression' was more accurate. In many respects, the debate about whether a black disabled person is oppressed on two separate counts or experiences simultaneous oppression (Stuart, 1992) is ultimately a dead end, since the sum total is still an oppressive experience.

It took some time for the organisations of disabled people to comprehend and acknowledge the extent of these cultural and identity differences however. There were some memorably vitriolic exchanges from the floor at conferences of the British Deaf Association with black members claiming that their views were ignored and that the executive did not represent their views (being entirely composed at the time of white people, nearly all men). These clashes were a regular occurrence until the time (several years later) when the realities of representation issues were seriously addressed.

In terms of professional practice with black and minority ethnic disabled people, there is still a dearth of specific literature that addresses cultural difference, although the core issues of particular oppressions based on ethnic difference are now included in most general debates concerning disabled people.

There is no doubt that statuses such as ethnicity, contribute to a substantially different experience for the disabled people in question. This is exemplified in the position of disabled refugees and asylum seekers (Roberts and Harris, 2001; Harris, 2003). A study of actual welfare entitlements and social conditions of disabled refugees and asylum seekers (Roberts and Harris, 2001) found that impairment is an invisible status in negotiations with those in power such as the Home Office and officers from the National Asylum Support Service (NASS). Impairment (or as they term it, disability) was not even catalogued in Home Office records at the time of the study and thus it proved impossible to know how many disabled asylum seekers were in the system.[2] This is an important

---

[2] The Home Office began collecting statistics on 'disability' following the study, partly as a result of political pressure exerted using the study as evidence.

point for those of us interested in the workings of the social policy system. If statistics on statuses and characteristics are not kept, requests for information (for example from MPs in the parliamentary process, or from researchers) cannot be answered. Black holes in knowledge are sometimes convenient for policy makers, but frustrate researchers and campaigners, especially those who wish to use evidence to improve economic and social conditions for oppressed groups.

Curiously, in the same study it was observed that the invisibilising of impairment had far-reaching consequences for disabled asylum seekers and refugees. For example, the dispersal policy took no account of support needs or language requirements of disabled asylum seekers. There were examples of people with mobility impairments dispersed to tower block accommodation on the third floor, with no means of getting to the only shop in the area that would exchange food vouchers. Whilst the report's authors did not suggest that this was deliberately inhumane treatment, it serves to demonstrate the monstrous consequences of invisibilising impairment.

Similarly, little account was taken of linguistic and cultural requirements, and in some cases, this had extreme effects. One participant in the study used Tamil sign language (Harris and Roberts, 2003) but there proved to be no interpreters with this skill in the UK. In these situations, it is hard to believe that the asylum seeker received full information, or was able to present their case to the Home Office on equal terms to non-disabled asylum seekers. There are complex and multifarious issues in relation to disabled asylum seekers; for example, a cataloguing system that ignored and disregarded impairment with often disastrous consequences and failed to appreciate cultural and linguistic specific requirements was a long way from a system of equality and fairness. Equally disturbing were the study's findings that disabled asylum seekers received little support from either asylum seekers organisations or organisations of disabled people. Instead, disabled refugees and asylum seekers seemed to fall between both provisions.

The current situation seems little improved. A study conducted in 2006 examined:

> ... the barriers faced by Black and minority ethnic (BME) people with sensory impairment along the whole employment journey, from education and training through to interviews and in the workplace. Most of all, this study points to the need to recognise that policy and practice are directed at either disability or ethnicity but rarely at both, failing to meet the needs of this most marginalised group. An integrated approach is required which also incorporates other forms of social division such as gender. Only in this way can we address discrimination of all kinds in a holistic manner. Our research participants argue strongly for this kind of integrated approach. For them, regardless of how they see their own identity – as people with impairments or as members of minority ethnic groups – it is often difficult to make sense of the discrimination that they encounter, although they are quite clear that discrimination occurs. Achieving the goal of integrated anti-discrimination practice will require

better collection of equality monitoring data, better training for staff in both attitudes and service delivery, more accessible practices and strong promotion of good practice, wherever it occurs. This will not be easy. The difficulties we had in conducting this study – in finding respondents and in gaining their trust – illustrate the difficulties that organisations will face. But face them they must if the Government's declarations on social exclusion are to go beyond mere rhetoric. Offering an analysis of the problems facing ethnic minority populations is one thing; doing something effective about it is quite another. (Ali et al., 2006: 1)

As long as services exist that categorise people primarily by impairment group and which fail to comprehend the intersection of statuses that result in oppression on secondary and tertiary grounds, we will continue to hear the complaint that services from Health and Social Care are not culturally sensitive and that this can result in inappropriate service provision:

Within disability organisations and within services, impairment can easily be seen as the main part of a person's identity, ignoring other aspects such as race, ethnicity, gender or class and caste.

As Mildrette Hill, founder of the Black Disabled People's Association, argues: They may have unique needs and wants, which cannot necessarily be met by services developed for white disabled people or for Black nondisabled people. There have been calls for more culturally sensitive or 'culturally competent' services, and for resources to support self-advocacy and disability awareness within minority communities. There has been concern about the provision of information and about communication at the point of service delivery. (Shah and Priestley, 2001: 6)

The project (Shah and Priestley, 2001) also found: 'concerns amongst minority disabled people about issues of diet, religious observance, gender roles, staffing, and trust. Local Black-led user groups have been more successful in making cultural competence work' (Shah and Priestley, 2001: 33). Inferior service provision with regard to information availability and barriers within the Health service was also found.

These are areas ripe for the development of positive practice. Practitioners can utilise the key findings of such studies and particularly can utilise the models in black people's own user-led organisations in order to produce culturally sensitive and useable outcomes with black and minority ethnic disabled people.

WHAT DO YOU THINK?

How can services and practitioners become more sensitive to the cultural and linguistic needs of black and minority ethnic disabled people?

Sexuality, sexual identity and parenting   ● ● ● ● ● ●

In the same way that 'ethnicity' was traditionally sidelined by disability studies, sexuality and sexual identity also had an extremely low profile. Disabled people were not seriously considered sexual beings pre-community care, and, as noted above, incarceration in institutions problematised the natural formation of sexual relationships (Shakespeare et al., 1996). As detailed above, the advent of community care meant that service providers had seriously to consider the prospect that disabled people want to have sexual relationships and furthermore, to have families.

The issue of disabled people's sexuality appears to make both professionals and the public uneasy. Few disabled writers traditionally wrote exclusively about sexual identity, with the exception of Tom Shakespeare. In relation to the 'body beautiful' stereotypes promulgated in the media, he writes:

> Rather than struggling to conform and to fit in to stereotypes, which developed on the basis of exclusivity and the body beautiful, and narrow, limited notions of how to behave and how to look, disabled people can challenge the obsession with fitness and youth and the body, and demonstrate that sexual activity and sexual attraction can be whatever you want it to be. (Shakespeare, 2000: 163)

This is sound advice for the vast majority of people who do not wish to dance to the media's tune. However, the stereotypes noted above are culturally embedded and therefore very difficult to dislodge. The work of challenging such stereotypes is difficult for individuals to undertake and is better done in our collectives and organisations. Professionals and practitioners have a distinct role here in raising awareness of these issues, modelling anti-discriminatory practice principles and challenging these stereotypes.

The key issues here surround not just sex and sexual identity but critically performance of that identity. This is an area in which the social model of disability fits very well. It is easy to see that there are few issues for disabled people in the performance of sexual identity that are not related in some way to the oppressive practices of non-disabled people, in particular, the ways in which the latter view the former. This has been explored in depth by Morris (1991 quoted in Swain et al. 1993: 102–3). For example, Morris details a number of key assumptions that are made about disabled people by non-disabled people:

> That we are asexual or at best sexually inadequate.

> That if we are not married or in a long-term relationship it is because no one wants us and not through our personal choice to remain single or live alone.

> That any able-bodied person who married us must have done so for one of the following suspicious motives and never through love: desire to hide his/her own inadequacies in the disabled partner's obvious ones; an altruistic and saintly desire to sacrifice their lives to our care; neurosis of some sort; or plain old-fashioned fortune-hunting.

That if we have a partner who is also disabled, we chose each other for no other reason and not for any other qualities we might possess. When we choose 'our own kind' in this way the able-bodied world feels relieved, until of course we wish to have children; then we're seen as irresponsible.

(Pam Evans in an interview with Morris [1991], quoted in Swain et al., 1993: 102–3)

Thus disabled women are oppressed by these and other views of the performance of sexuality and sexual identity by non-disabled societal members. As a positive practitioner, the key issue here is to recognise the oppressive practices and thoughts that disabled women encounter and challenge these at every opportunity. Expect to encounter opposition to your approach; stigmatisation and hate-crime have deep roots.

If the issue of sexuality and the performance of sexual identity makes professionals uneasy, parenting arguably induces even stronger responses. There is a small but growing literature on disabled parenting, much of it developed by Michelle Wates, who has written extensively about the issues disabled parents face, such as mainstream societal disapproval and, explicitly, society's failure to comprehend how disabled parents can care for their children, historically stemming from pigeonholing them as 'dependent' themselves (Wates, 1997).

Some literature on disabled parents is centrally concerned with housing issues (Sapey et al., 2005). Wates (2003) and Disabled Parents Network (2005) indicate that one of the issues to be considered is that whilst disabled parents may have a greater need than other disabled people to access all areas of their homes, some find that local authorities are not prepared to consider their needs in relation to meeting the needs of children. If parents are to supervise their children's activities they will need this access, whereas it may be more acceptable to other disabled people who are not parents that some areas are inaccessible. There is a similarity here to the additional housing requirements identified by Beresford and Oldman (2002) in relation to disabled children. They highlight issues such as play space and the local environment as factors which impact on the experiences of families with disabled children, although these are not factors that might traditionally be considered by planners and architects.

There has been a long-standing claim within disability studies that universal, rather than a 'special needs' approach to disability policy should be pursued in recognition that the entire population is at risk from the effects of chronic illness and disability (Sapey et al. 2005; Zola, 1989). The idea of accessible 'Lifetime Homes' in the UK (Bonnett, 1996; Cobbold, 1997) draws on this universalised approach and assumes that it is reasonable for all people to stay in their own homes regardless of changes in their physical ability. The UK amendment to the Building Regulations (Part M) is a way of beginning to operationalise this approach which should in the long-term result in inclusive solutions. This is good news for all families that include or may at some point include disabled members.

Evidence from several housing studies (Harris, Sapey and Stewart 1997a, 1997b; Sapey, 1995; Sapey et al., 2004; Stewart et al., 1999) indicates that disabled people want to choose whether or not to move home, and if they do wish to move they want choice. This situation is no different for disabled parents. Indeed there is evidence to suggest that disabled parents have additional factors to consider when deciding whether to stay put and where to live (Olsen and Clarke, 2002; Wates, 1997).

The issue here is that the 'special needs' approach to the housing needs of disabled parents adopted in policy and practice terms is a dead end. It has led to well-meaning practice solutions such as databases of accessible homes, on the assumption that disabled people who wish to move can swap with each other. However, the need for such databases only arises because of the lack of a universalist approach and the adoption of a 'Lifetime Homes' mentality. It is only through the adoption of a universalised approach that choice will be achieved, not through the development of more databases which are simply part of a centralised planning ethos that paternalistically assumes that politicians and administrators are better placed to make decisions on behalf of disabled people.

WHAT DO YOU THINK?

Consider the issues raised by disability and sexuality. Do these issues cause you concern?

Make a list of all the issues that you are concerned about on the left hand side of a piece of paper. Afterwards, on the right hand side, write whether your concerns are based on personal, ethical or moral considerations. Put a star beside any that you feel raise potential issues of protection or abuse. Put the list away for a week and then reappraise your decisions.

Conclusion

In this chapter we considered how to value diversity and looked at key issues relating to mental health, which included consideration of the ground covered since the revolution inspired by the community care legislation and the ensuing policy and practice roll out.

We have considered learning disability, especially issues of difference and societal pressures to conform to visible and stereotypical ideas of beauty, and we have examined ethnicity, focusing particularly on issues relating to disabled refugees and asylum seekers and acknowledging that the ways in which people are counted can affect whether services are put in place to respond to identified 'need'.

The gendered nature of 'care' is a fact, the issue is only how a positive practitioner should approach it. We have seen also that disabled women experience specific issues at various points across the life course, particularly in employment and ageing. A positive practitioner seeks to understand these key areas and work with disabled women in countering the oppressive practices of non-disabled people.

In discussing sexuality and parenting, we have seen how these topics have historically been areas that make professionals uneasy and in some cases, more likely to adopt defensive practice. However, defensive practice and 'special needs' approaches, as we have seen in relation to housing, are dead ends both in policy and practice terms. Universalist approaches and Lifetime Homes fit both with the social model of disability and common sense in that, in the long run, they will result in accessible environments and alleviate the necessity of moving for impairment issues.

In terms of the diversity of disabled people as a whole, until recently, disability studies has not embraced the core issues. Partly this situation can be seen to have arisen from the initial focus upon issues that unite rather than those which divide. However, identities and expression are key aspects of all disabled people's lives and diversity points up the challenges of developing services that can meet them. Every situation is different and must be approached in a spirit of valuing diversity.

Further reading

Mansell J., Knapp M., Beadle-Brown, J. and Beecham, J. (2007) *Deinstitutionalisation and Community Living – Outcomes and Costs: Report of a European Study. Volume 1: Executive Summary*. Canterbury: Tizard Centre.

Priestley, M. (2003) *Disability: A Life Course Approach*. Cambridge: Polity.

Roulstone, A. and Thomas, P. (2009) *Hate Crime and Disabled People*. Equality and Human Rights Commission and Breakthrough UK, Manchester.

8

Key Challenges for an Aspiring Social Model Practitioner

Introduction

In this chapter we examine key challenges for an aspiring practitioner wishing to use the social model of disability and ask what are the likely barriers and facilitators to positive practice. We begin with a look at the challenge of user control and choice and ways of approaching these issues for social model practitioners. This is followed by 'managing the managers' – a critical look at budgetary constraints and street-level bureaucracy, where we examine in detail how practitioners approach dealing with a disempowering system.

We will then turn to the complex issues of 'mental capacity and power of attorney', and ask how can the social worker's duty of care be balanced with social model practice? This is followed by an exploration of the benefits of working with colleagues in user-led organisations, and we then go on to discuss the context within which practice is situated and the centrality of the disabled person.

Finally, we ask how professionals can develop 'real reflexivity' in working with disabled people.

The challenge of user control and choice: how should a social model practitioner act?

Successive legislation has incorporated user control and choice as central to the production of quality service provision to disabled people (DoH, 2005a). In fact, the extent of user control and choice are hallmarks of good quality services.

However, producing real user control and choice is not easy, particularly within the restrictive frameworks of statutory service provision. Since social model approaches all have in common the key features of barriers and facilitators, it is useful here to use this framework. Firstly what are the key barriers for service providers attempting to act as social model practitioners?

It must be remembered here, that the UK disability movement was born from dissatisfaction with the existing status quo of services, which too often were produced within a paternalistic framework that gave disabled people little or no say in services or care. As we have seen, community care as a policy and as a guiding principle for delivering services has taken a considerable time to bed down and this is largely because it represents an almost total reversal of service provision philosophy prior to its introduction. The first barrier therefore is this historical legacy and attitudes that have been entrenched in service provision from that time.

Secondly, in terms of control over service input and outcome, victories are hard won by disabled people and it would be wrong to suggest that the battles are all fought, especially in regard to the issues of professionalism and expert power (cf. Harris et al., 2005). Talking about the 'empowerment' of service users is much easier than producing empowering services, because giving away control means giving away power. Once professionals give away power, they feel undone as professionals. Similarly, giving service users choice can evoke fear in some professionals, largely because they imagine that service users will ask for items that either they cannot produce or, more to the point, cannot afford (Harris et al., 2005). The professional must then attempt to justify the costs of these large or expensive items to the service manager. However, research suggests that neither is the case in reality and these professional fears are unfounded (Harris et al., 2005). Disabled people readily accept that there are budgetary limits and do not make unreasonable requests for items from service providers (Harris et al., 2005). The second barrier, therefore, is professional power that is founded upon notions of 'expertise'. The question becomes, how can practitioners work with disabled people within a relationship of mutual respect and equality, rather than as expert or professional and client? Many insights may be gained through joint working with disabled people in user-led organisations. These organisations work on a practical philosophy of equality inspired by the social model of disability. Strong and rigid hierarchies, such as those set up and maintained traditionally within social services, do not exist in the same ways. Contact with user-led organisation members will always result in heightened appreciation of user perspectives and more equitable ways of working with disabled people.

Where does this leave the 'social model practitioner'? A social model practitioner will experience contradictions from the outset owing to their commitment to the social model (which states that disabled people are oppressed by the non-disabled majority and which acknowledges those in power as part of the problem rather than part of the solution) (Swain et al., 1993; 2004). The attempt to make professional services better or based upon empowering principles, would to some seem futile – services that are based upon 'intervention' in disabled people's lives cannot, under such a view, be improved and would be better disbanded.

However, given the status quo and the existing policy and service system that we have, disabled people for the foreseeable future will come into contact with professionals from Health and Social Care services. Within this given status quo, we ask what facilitators are there for the aspiring social model practitioner? Undoubtedly, many professionals involved in the production of services to disabled people do act in respectful, considerate and understanding ways and certainly do not seek to patronise or remove control from disabled people. The first facilitator therefore is what was historically called reflexive practice or self-monitoring (Taylor and White, 2006). This useful skill has become somewhat out of fashion in recent years but formed part of the armoury of those professionals engaged in person-centred practice, currently now very much in vogue once again (Taylor and White, 2006).

Reflexive practice at its core is about consideration – both considering what one is doing in working with the person, and, more critically, how one is doing it and how it is being received. The 'do as you would be done by' mentality at the heart of this skill is certainly useful for starters. Any act that gives disabled people more control over the process and production of their services and the practitioner less control can be taken as a rudimentary marker of success.

The second facilitator concerns commitment to producing a service that embodies real choice for users. Where service quality is poor, this is difficult from the outset. Giving users a choice between two inferior services over which they have no control, effectively is no choice at all. This is why Direct Payments score so highly over services provided by professionals, since users can control what, when and where inputs are made, and critically make discerning decisions concerning service quality (Prideaux et al., 2009). Offering service users who prefer not to use Direct Payments real choice means sourcing various options and respecting and implementing the service user's decision on which they prefer. It is possible to see here though that in situations where the only service(s) available are low quality, the professional has little hope of assisting the service user to achieve the high quality outcome that is desired. This is a point at which the aspirations of disabled people do not match with the resources available from statutory service providers, which can be a constant source of frustration.

Despite the difficulties, the principles of real user choice and control are extremely important and indeed these underpin the personalisation agenda. Service users always prefer to choose and control service provision, even when the choice is limited, and even when control may be somewhat compromised by inferior quality. Retaining choice and control is vital in such situations, since 'consumer power' works to improve service quality and the extent of real control.

Thirdly, even when they are paid by statutory authorities, professionals have an important role in advocating for high quality service provision on behalf of service users and using their professional power to demand improvements in service quality. Various policies in place, such as the Best Value initiative, support professionals in this endeavour. Too often, professionals appear to believe that to criticise poor practice or service delivery leaves them vulnerable to discrimination at the hands of their superior officers. However, ultimately, all providers of services are answerable to the people they serve and it is in the superior officers' best interests to promote and maintain high quality service provision. Using the above guidance, professional power can be used to positive, rather than negative effect.

Managing the managers – budgetary constraints and street level bureaucracy: dealing with a disempowering system

If this book had been written before the 1990 NHS and Community Care Act, the section on management and disability would have painted a very different picture of disability support services and management. Firstly the term management would have been closely associated with senior and middle positions in a support/care hierarchy. The term 'management' can be seen to have been broadened to embrace senior, middle managers, frontline professionals and also unqualified social and health care workers in the form of care management. Care management has also widened its remit, and those holding the post of care manager may have trained in social care, nursing, occupational therapy and/or related disciplines (DoH, 2006). Before 1990, the provision of services would have been clearly demarcated in health, social care, rehabilitation, employment services, despite disabled people long arguing that their needs were not so easily compartmentalised (DoH, 2006). Much has happened since the mid-1990s to challenge these ideas in practice and policy terms, as we have explored above.

The idea of the 'management' of care and support services for disabled people some 20 years on is then a much more diverse affair. The notion of management of 'care' can be construed as frontline working from (un)qualified practitioners through to the activities of directors of social service departments, Primary Care Trusts, housing departments and Jobcentre Plus. This section does not aim to provide a 'state of the art' picture of management in the above areas nor their professional standing per se, indeed these are well rehearsed in existing published sources (Manthorpe and Bradley in Adams et al., 2009: 204–12; Weinberg et al., 2003).

Given the changing policy and programme environment, we construe the 'management of disabled people' for the purposes of this discussion as any professional (qualified or not) actively engaged with disabled service users who can influence the allocation of services, goods and financial transactions. This is not to argue that unqualified social work assistants acting as care managers have anything substantively in common with a director of social services, indeed nuanced professional cues will be provided which reflect these differences. However, as the development towards a single 'spine' of care work embodied in the General Social Care Council (GSCC) symbolised, workers at all levels have a role to play in the management and delivery of services. In this sense management is taken to mean a formalised paid role in supporting disabled people to maximise health, opportunity and mainstreamed lives. The principal concern here relates to the challenge for managers of enhanced partnership in working with disabled people, both the challenge of working within a given service and across service providers. The issue of coordination of services is central to more enabling services for disabled people in contemporary society.

At its most ambitious the Every Child Matters agenda (DfES, 2003), Aiming High (HM Treasury and DCfS, 2007) in children's services and Personalisation and Self-Directed Support (DoH, 2005a) are providing momentum towards disabled people taking greater control over their own lives in the receipt and use of funding through direct payments in adult social care. This of course ushers in the spectre of joined-up services, co-location and joint commissioning in disabled children's services. In adult services, the imagery is perhaps yet more dramatic, with disabled people managing increasing aspects of their lives, challenging the traditional professionally embedded meaning of 'management' of care and support.

One disability organisation has captured this in its name: 'Being the Boss' (http://www.beingtheboss.co.uk/) and indeed recent policy and practice changes call for a wholesale change in thinking as to just what management and 'being the boss' is taken to mean. This should not however, obscure the paradoxical situation that these inspirational and important changes to adult social care are taking place in an environment of funding constraints (Aldgate et al., 2007; LGA and ADSS, 2006) and that for now, middle and senior managers still hold a pivotal position as resource gatekeepers. This gatekeeping role has major implications for the more general management of support for disabled people. The role, vision and efficacy of managers at all levels is central to the effective development of self-directed support; one underpinned by good financial foundations and a joined-up approach to rolling out personalisation approaches. A failure to match new ideas with these wider supports will lead to the enforced individualism of disabled people (Roulstone and Morgan, 2009).

Although this book is largely concerned with disability policy and related practice, in the arena of management it is important to frame practice in the wider shifts in public sector management and what some writers call the 'new public management'. Although interpretations of these shifts vary, the core features of new public management are:

- Devolved budgetary cultures and structures
- Financial planning at the heart of wider planning protocols
- Emphasis on value for money (e.g. in Best Value projects)
- Shift towards general management.

(Clarke et al., 2000)

A close reading of 'new public management' suggests that these policies might be at odds with the philosophy of equality, personalisation, choices and rights. Managers and frontline professionals need to be aware of these possible tensions (Riddell et al., 2006) and must offer creative solutions to these by challenging at street level (Lipsky, 1980) the application of financially-driven models of social support.

One way to begin to tackle the tensions laid out above is to be alert to and to avoid diluting the original principles of key practice developments. For example, personalisation began life as a broad philosophical commitment to greater self direction, but also aimed at 'reducing loneliness and isolation, increasing inter-generational activity, investing in community services ... ' (Manthorpe cited in Mickel, 2008).

Independence, Wellbeing and Choice (DoH, 2005a) and *Our Health, Our Care, Our Say* (DoH, 2006) also exhort professionals to aid preventive measures, for example avoiding needless institutionalisation, injury or risks to public safety. In this way senior managers and middle managers with strategic positions locally (for example on partnership boards, Learning Disability Partnership Boards, Health Trusts and Crime Reduction Strategy Boards) have the opportunity to embed preventive strategies.

These wider facets of personalisation have arguably been overshadowed by self-directed support ideas which could result in assistance becoming unduly individualised if not supported by the wider points of personalisation. Personalisation should not be reduced to a 'salad bar' approach which addresses exclusively the immediate issues of personal choice and overlooks the continued contribution to a safe, secure, accepting society, the absence of which would make a mockery of a choices and rights agenda.

Managers working with disabled people need to understand the important distinction between individual choice-making and tailored support at the heart of personalisation and individualisation (Roulstone and Morgan, 2009), which in its purest form equals complete self reliance and which is not only unattainable, but also does violence to the original conception of personalisation. Interdependency remains at the heart of social relationships between community members. This can be overlooked in some interpretations of self-directed support.

It is important to ensure that social care workers at all levels engage with accessible and safe transport issues, community safety issues in public and institutional contexts (e.g. day centres), enabling and disabling aspects of the health care system. Challenges can be drawn out in terms of hierarchical and sectoral ideas.

There is a growing literature on the challenges of bringing together stakeholders and managers within a given professional context to support more enabling provision and practice. For example, work by the Care Services Improvement Partnership (CSIP, 2007) points to the tensions of health service driven targets to reduce acute care waiting lists, which in turn risks playing down the more preventative aspects of *Independence, Wellbeing and Choice* (DoH, 2005a). Writing in a Scottish context, Disability Concern note the need for staff at all levels in the health service to work together and with disabled people creatively to: '... promote a culture of enquiry, creative thought and change amongst health service professionals and managers ... Encourage frontline staff to put forward ideas and facilitate adoption of those [ideas] that are promising' (Disability Concern Glasgow, 2007). The wider article points out the urgent need for health authorities to implement fully and flexibly the social care legislation of the last 20 years. Engagement with these policies at the highest levels in the health service remains a challenge, and it is difficult to envisage good practice at the front line with disabled people where more senior staff have still to place disability and social support on their own radar. There are ways to help frontline staff embrace the personalisation agenda by drawing from parallel developments – for example the Expert Patient programme which draws on similar models of self direction and active involvement in service review.

In the social work context there is evidence of very different perspectives between senior management and operational staff with adult social care being increasingly squeezed by fiscal and demographic factors (Aldgate et al., 2007; LGA and ADSS, 2006). Senior managers have of necessity to take the wider view on meeting the needs of all disabled people deemed eligible for support, whilst being mindful of the new Resource Allocation (RAS) approach being adopted.

Duffy (2008) notes that the reluctance of some senior managers to support the wholesale growth of direct payments further hampers shifts towards self-directed working. Direct payments, personalisation and individual budgets are likely to become more rather than less important in adult social care given demographic shifts (CSIP, 2007) which suggests that the signals around the expansion of self-directed support need to increasingly be seen to come from the senior management team in a social services department.

A rather worrying piece of research recently reported in *Community Care*, the 'house journal' for social care professionals, pointed to the preponderance of social workers who believed that personalisation, as it is currently constructed, risks making social care service users more rather than less vulnerable. Indeed without wider community safety and transport measures in place and without sufficient key worker support for the most vulnerable people, the position is an understandable one. However, it is imperative that the idea of personalisation continues to receive 'primary billing' in adult social care planning.

Problems of implementation should not be conflated with inherent problems with the concept of personalisation and self-directed support. There are ways in which managers at all levels can support frontline staff in fostering best practice in personalisation – for example in pushing forward on self assessment and not assuming that self assessment is a step too far – as the shift to moderated assessments in some local authorities seems to suggest. The latest ideas in developing the adult social care agenda point to the role and potential of co-production of services between disabled people and frontline care workers (SCIE, 2008). This is a goal that if realised would symbolise the maturing of the personalisation agenda.

A corresponding requirement of enabling professional support is the successful pooling of efforts across health, social care, employment, housing and community safety services. The recent study by Erwin-Jones (2008) provides some promising results, with 88% of respondent professionals saying they supported shared support approaches to service provision. In reality it is rarely a principled objection to working with other sector professionals that stands in the way of shared working and support. In truth it is more likely professional confidentiality thresholds and spatial and budgetary issues that lead to poor coordination.

The shift to a Single Assessment Process (SAP) (Whittam, 2007) is one clear example of this challenge. There is much evidence of the existence of hierarchies of credibility and professional standing at the point where health and social care workers interface with each other. The Modernising Adult Social Care (MASC) research programme, a major review of the field (Newman, 2007), looked at the processes and outcomes of contemporary adult social care services. The study found evidence of the 'hegemony' of the health paradigm in areas of adult social care working. This is also evident in the context of the new Approved Mental Health Practitioner, where although access to the role can emanate from a range of health and social care professions, the perception amongst some social care professionals is that health professionals have been seen to have 'greater credibility' in this context (Roulstone and Morgan, 2009). This cannot be helpful in aiding inter-professional working (Newman, 2007; see also Roulstone and Hudson, 2007).

Managers in health and social care need to be alive to this challenge, to encourage and personally engage with joint working and do their bit to reduce hierarchies. Similarly, research by the Voluntary Organisations Disability Group (VODG, 2007) points to the delays in disabled people moving home each year because of poor joint working protocols between PCTs and local authority housing departments based on disputes around who should fund a disabled person's social care. Clearly frontline workers can only have a limited impact in breaking down such service barriers, whilst managers may be better placed to exploit health and social care flexibilities to more effectively support disabled peoples' wider needs. Indeed, flexible working can save money, as is the case where housing adaptations funded through the Disabled Facilities Grant can help avoid needless institutionalisation or prolonged discharge from acute healthcare or intermediate care settings (Henwood and Turner, 2007)

Mental capacity and Power of Attorney: how can the duty of care be balanced with social model practice?

The issue of mental capacity is central to humane and enabling working with disabled people. As we saw in previous chapters, having an obvious impairment or difference has historically led to the categorical exclusion from mainstream life and to the curtailment of freedoms non-disabled people have taken for granted (Foucault, 2001; Stiker, 2000). At times of social crisis, when, for example, a person could not make decisions for themselves or were perceived not to be able to, blanket assumptions were often made that control should shift to professionals or close family members. Even temporary incapacity was often taken as a pretext to withdraw longer-term control and decision-making. Notions that professionals should speak for disabled people, particularly people with dementia and significant mental health problems, have arguably been pervasive and at times harmful (Brandon and Hawkes, 1998).

Decisions as to whether to accept medical treatment, the disposal of personal and financial assets and, in extremis, the refusal to accept food are central to the question of capacity and control. Conversely, for those with learning difficulties, professional decisions not to continue medical treatment, feeding or the sustaining of life have also raised key issues as to when a person is or is not capable of deciding on their affairs.

The recent passage of the Human Rights Act (2000) has helped reinforce public and professional sentiment that disabled people have inalienable legal and human rights whatever their wider circumstances. There are, however, some very genuine and important situations in which capacity is a reasonable issue for professional judgement. For example, a person with dementia who has no close relatives and who needs support to help with financial and accommodation issues, or a person who is threatening suicide and who is a risk to themselves or others but who wants to make key decisions which could impact their lives significantly. These require a good grasp of capacity-related legislation. The recent passage of the Mental Capacity Act (2005) has helped to strengthen protections and to clarify the appropriate intervention to make both to safeguard personal rights but also to minimise further harm or distress to an individual.

The Mental Capacity Act (2005) is not entirely new, and some commentators have described the Act as a consolidation of existing common law (case by case) protections (see Brayne and Martin, 1999: 343–5; BMA and Law Society, 2007). More than this, the Act is pivotal as a Statute (HM Government, 2005), Guidance (DoH, 2007e) and training set (DoH, 2007d) in aiding professionals to make the correct decisions by providing pointers to good practice in capacity decisions. The case law approach was arguably a lawyers' charter and was only activated once a problem was identified. Lawyers have not exited the scene in terms of capacity issues, but it is hoped that by disseminating good principles and practices, only the most complex and/or contested issues of capacity will need to reach the courts.

The Mental Capacity Act was the result of a very protracted process, with statutory attention being paid to the issue from the 1990s with the advent of the Law Commission Enquiry in 1995. The perception that primary legislation was required became encapsulated in the 2004 Draft Mental Health Bill (DoH, 2004c). The Mental Capacity Act (MCA) (2005) became operational from 2007 and its provisions were rolled out that year. The MCA can be seen to connect fundamental legal rights (National Council for Palliative Care, 2007) to humane treatment reflecting the diversity of disabled peoples' circumstances. In this sense the Act draws on notions of person-centred planning (DoH, 2000a) and latterly personalisation (DoH, 2005a; 2008d).

Following much policy and practice in the era of *Valuing People* and *Independence, Wellbeing and Choice*, a person assessed for capacity is to be located at the centre of the process to decide on capacity, whatever the outcome of that process. The need for the Mental Capacity Act is laid out in the following foreword to the MCA Core Training Guidance aimed at health and social care professionals:

> The new MCA will play an important part in safeguarding and protecting those people in society who lack capacity to do so for themselves. Working in health and social care, you will be playing a vital part in supporting and caring for some of the most vulnerable people in society and I am confident that you will rise to the challenge posed by the new MCA. (DoH, 2007d)

In substantive terms, where such rights are not protected and decisions are taken against the wishes of a disabled or incapacitated person two new criminal offences have been created: (1) ill treatment; and (2) wilful neglect. These provisions then are in place where capacity issues have been actively exploited or where severe cases of neglect are in evidence. Much the rest of the Act's provisions relate to positive and proactive interventions that respect issues of capacity and incapacity. The MCA is accompanied by a Code of Practice on capacity that lays out key principles and definitions:

> Based on available evidence the following are seen as likely causes of incapacity: Permanent and temporary lack of capacity due to dementia, organic brain or neurological disease, mental illness, severe frailty, learning difficulty. Of great significance those working with people perceived to have limited mental capacity must not make sweeping judgements and a significant factor is the objective and professionally agreed measure of impairment/functioning. (For a fuller legal statement see the Mental Capacity Act 'Code of Practice' (Department of Constitutional Affairs, 2007)

The UK government estimates that there are between 1 and 2 million adults who at a given time might lack capacity (DoH, 2007d: 8; Learning Set). The Code applies to those over 16 years and makes clear that if capacity is temporary and adjudged to alter over a short period of time, the Code's guidance is to attempt wherever possible to defer decision making (see BMA and Law Society, 2007). Where capacity is deemed absent, substitute decision makers can be nominated under the 'Lasting Power of Attorney' provision.

Under Sections 1–4 of the MCA, the test for capacity set out in the Code of Practice establishes a two-stage capacity test as follows:

1   Is there an impairment of or disturbance of the person's mind or brain?
2   Is the impairment or disturbance sufficient that a person lacks capacity to make a given decision?

The Code makes clear, the task or event-specific nature of capacity as it is to be judged and this signals a rejection of and reaction to previously categorical and blanket judgements that have established capacity 'once and for all' and used the judgement of capacity uncritically in future treatments. The basic tenets of the MCA are displayed below:

A presumption of capacity: the five principles of capacity assessment

- A person is assumed to have capacity unless it is established otherwise.
- A person is not treated as unable to make a decision unless all practicable steps to help have been taken without success.
- A person is not treated as unable to make a decision merely because they make (or might be seen likely to make) an unwise decision.
- Decisions must be in the 'best interests' of the person who lacks capacity.
- Before the act is done (in establishing incapacity) or the decision is made, regard must be had to whether the purpose for which it is needed can be effectively achieved in a way that is less restrictive of the person's rights and freedom of action.

(DoH, 2007e)

The assessment of capacity therefore should take into account whether the person:

1   Can understand the information/issues relevant to given decision
2   Can absorb/retain that information – for example where a decision may be delayed
3   Can weigh up evidence in making a decision
4   Is able to communicate a decision.

In the Learning Set materials provided by the Department of Health (DoH, 2007d) they provide the example of a person being able to communicate consent by 'blinking an eye or squeezing a hand' (DoH, 2007d: 10). If a person fails one or more of these tests this allows a finding of incapacity.

In coming to a decision, the Code of Practice attaches a 'best interest test' to decisions as to capacity. In deciding whether something is in an individual's best interest, their current views, family circumstances and views, family records and/ or living wills should be taken into account. Additionally a person's beliefs and values should be taken into account.

Decisions should where possible involve family, friends and other professionals. Lasting Power of Attorney nominee or deputy of the Court of Protection are used where risks would attach to involving any close relatives or friends (see Department of Constitutional Affairs, 2007). Exceptional circumstances attach to decisions where issues of loss of liberty are at stake, for example where a section of the Mental Health Act might otherwise be invoked (Department of Constitutional Affairs, 2007: 97–8).

This exception was established in the Bournewood Decision (Crichton, 1998) and is a safeguard which ensures that the fullest legal considerations are given where lack of capacity could lead to an unduly detrimental decision as to custodial sanctions. Here, applications must in all instances be made to a supervisory body (DoH, 2007e) which is usually taken to mean a local authority or PCT. This ruling reflects the safeguards set out in the Human Rights Act (2000) which can sit awkwardly with compulsory sections of the Mental Health Acts (Daw, 2003).

To date, there has been evidence of the Mental Health Amendment Bill being implemented to ensure that in instances where mental capacity and detention are both at stake, but patients are compliant, a supervisory body must supervene. Some cases had to be taken to legal proceedings *ab initio*, for example: where nutrition may be withheld; where there is a proposal for non-therapeutic sterilisation; in certain proposed terminations of pregnancy; and where medical care is in the patient's best interests and is severely contested (BMA and Law Society, 2007).

Assessment must be undertaken by the professional attached to an individual's case unless an advocacy service is explicitly involved. The exact role of advocacy in capacity issues is still being tested, but given the wider shift to advocacy in the personalisation agenda it might be predicted that advocacy will likely increase in this area, especially where family and friends are not in evidence to help make decisions about capacity. To this end, the Independent Medical Capacity Advocate Service (IMCA) will be drawn on to support those with no obvious external community or family supports. Indeed, early evidence points to the concerns that even close family and friends have expressed that they may not be best placed to understand issues of capacity and that the IMCA is a useful safeguard (DoH, 2007d: 5 Training Set).

Capacity is of course a complex issue and assumptions should never be made based on rough 'global' assessments of capacity, for example a person with a learning difficulty may be able to make everyday choices as to whether they go out, what they eat, who they spend time with. If, however, a decision is made never to go out, or to go out unaccompanied or with insufficient clothing for inclement weather, an assessment of capacity should be undertaken (see DoH, 2007d: 11).

Capacity is contextual therefore and should take account of skills, attributes, levels of awareness of danger, recent decision-making and the reasons a person gives for making such a decision. Capacity decisions should largely be undertaken by the 'decision maker' who works day-to-day with a person and who is best placed to make such decisions. This would usually be social care staff in care settings and health care staff in a clinical setting. At times these requirements may need to be flexible where, for example, a health issue arises outside such a context. As ever, common sense should prevail in establishing whether a capacity issue is at stake and which person should lead the assessment. As a general rule, the more significant the decision, the more professional involvement there needs to be. It is also important to be aware that there are specific exemptions to this principle where the 'person is making or planning to make a will, gift, enter litigation, contract or marriage' (DoH, 2007d: 18).

These matters have to be dealt with under common law and not the MCA and thus require specialist professional advice. Where decisions are being made by a person that relate to sexual relationships, divorce, adoption or voting, these issues cannot be treated under the terms of the Mental Capacity Act as such decisions cannot be handed over under British law. Where a personal decision may be harmful or risky, expert legal and safeguarding advice needs to be sought. However it is absolutely essential in an era of personalisation not to make blanket assumptions as to lack of capacity. A careful assessment of personal rights and risks needs to be made. You may find the detailed examples of capacity decision-making in the Department of Health's Core Training Set helpful (DoH, 2007d).

Research into the effectiveness and impact of the MCA is in its early stages given the recent accession of the MCA to the statute book. However, a small number of studies have been completed, most notably the Sawhney et al. (2009) study for the Royal College of Psychiatrists which found a very mixed picture. Sixty-one per cent of respondents (practising psychiatrists) felt patient care had improved because of the safeguards laid out in the Act and the clarity of its guidance. In all, 79% of respondents felt their training in MCA matters was 'adequate'. However, aspects of the Act and its Guidance remained unclear for many, especially where new roles and functions had been introduced. For example, 81% of respondents were unaware when a person had to be referred to the Mental Capacity Advocate Service (IMCA), whilst 47% of respondents did not know that the MCA does not cover those under the terms of the 'Bournewood case'. This is somewhat concerning, but reflects the impact of ambitious new legislation such as the Mental Capacity Act.

The recently published Core Training Set (DoH, 2007d) goes some way to responding to the requirements of the Act and provides very helpful examples of appropriate actions and referrals when mental capacity issues arise.

Practice guidance summarised

The above suggests that the new Mental Capacity Act and its Guidance require a quantum shift in working with disabled people in the following ways:

- An assumption of capacity unless non-capacity can be established
- That blanket judgements about capacity based on stereotyped ideas of a given impairment or behaviour have to be rejected
- That creative and sensitive ways of trying to establish capacity need to be adopted and a recognition that to date professionals have often erred on the side of denying capacity is required
- That where capacity cannot be exercised in day-to-day decisions, individuals should still be treated with dignity and respect
- That where a judgement is made that capacity may be absent temporarily then a decision should where possible be deferred on capacity and that self-determination should be exercised at a later point
- That in instances where key life or highly personal decisions are being made (for example around relationships and money), joined up professional working and the appropriate use of legal safeguards is adopted.

Working with colleagues in user-led organisations

A significant development over the time since the advent of community care has been the rise of user-controlled organisations. From humble beginnings, these have blossomed and expanded their roles to be significant players in the disability arena. Pre-community care, most organisations involved with disabled people took an administrative approach. Most of these organisations were run as charities by non-disabled people who, although well meaning, could hardly claim epistemological privilege or identify centrally with disabled people's day-to-day issues. Such organisations can be seen as natural developments from the early philanthropic endeavours harking back as far as the Charitable Organisation Society (see Chapter 2). However, following this phase, in the modern era, we have seen the development of welfare rights organisations for disabled people (such as the Disability Income Group) who campaigned successfully on single-focus issues.

User-led organisations are a much newer innovation and can be seen as an indicator that the disability movement has come of age. A key player has been the

Centres for Independent Living (CIL), which began as a campaigning organisation (which function it still carries) and has expanded into a network of linked centres across the UK (see http://www.ncil.org.uk/). CILs explicitly use the social model of disability and aim to assist disabled people who wish to use direct payments or individual budgets. Some CILs have expanded their roles to include administration of direct payments, alleviating disabled people of the necessity of employing personal assistants.

These are therefore, exciting developments which are at the cutting edge of service provision to disabled people. Self-directed support, as promulgated and produced by these groups, is the way forward in both policy and practice terms. There are many ways in which professionals can learn from colleagues in user-led organisations. Firstly, the types of service and support developed to date are intrinsically in tune with disabled people's service requirements. Thus, you will not find stigmatising practices, such as labelling or concentration upon the impairment or condition, rather than disabling barriers. Secondly, assistance extended within these organisations is personalised to the individual without making this the focus of attention. Thus the individual will never lose their choice or control, both key factors. Finally, any professional wishing to understand the workings of self-directed support would be well advised to seek out their nearest CIL, as these groups were the early pioneers and are set to carry on innovating in this area.

Users, carers and wider service providers: seeing disabled people in context – the central place of the disabled person

Although the relationship between disabled people and professionals is at the heart of this book, in reality this relationship relies and in many cases depends upon the input from many other people: carers, families and third sector organisations.

When the social model was being established in the early 1990s, there was the feeling that carers' issues, such as their requirements for breaks and the acknowledgement of their stress, should not be foregrounded since this detracted from the spotlight upon the disabled person's oppression by mainstream society. This led to a rather unfair situation, where carers were effectively invisible and where ostensibly, it appeared the disability movement were claiming oppression, whilst failing to acknowledge the oppression of the people supporting them.

Although it is true to say this feeling has never entirely gone away, the problematisation of the social model and the critiques on the grounds of race and sex in particular, have widened the debate on the various statuses which result in oppression. To a large extent, this has enabled carers' issues to be acknowledged in a rudimentary fashion at least. What then are the main issues for carers that professionals should be addressing?

Undoubtedly, the issue of 'respite' care raises its head in any such discussion. The disability movement has had a problem with the whole issue of 'respite' care historically on several grounds. One of the main problems is that the carers' literature is largely produced by medics or professionals allied to medicine, who see little problem in discussing levels of 'burden' and 'carer stress' without exercising any consideration for the effect that this has upon perceptions of disabled people. The burgeoning literature on 'carer burden' and the search for an adequate tool to 'measure' it is testimony to this lack of regard.

Leaving issues of nomenclature aside for one moment, there is little point in disputing that some caring produces stress (Matson, 1994) whatever way you look at it, and that this stress is exacerbated by, and in some cases the result of, poverty (Glendinning and Kemp, 2006), discrimination and, in many cases (since women make up the majority of both paid and informal carers), sexism. Although not the focus of this book, the acknowledgement of the effects of care work upon carers is therefore a subject of magnitude which inspires strong feelings, both inside and outside of the Disabled Peoples' Movement.

One of the problems with the original social model of disability (Oliver, 1990) was that it isolated the disabled person from the carer in order to produce clarity in the argument concerning oppression. In reality, in situations where informal care is produced by a close family member in the community, the relationship between the disabled person and carer is a dyad; both are equally likely to be oppressed and equally likely to have unacknowledged and unmet service requirements, and the poverty that such dyads face through the inadequacies of the benefit system is equally deleterious to both parties.

What is required is a service delivery system that acknowledges the disabled person's requirements, that places choice and control by them at the centre of good quality service provision and that respects their rights to exercise choice and control in all matters. This does not mean, however, that carers have to be made invisible, or their rights ignored, in order to produce the latter situation. Carers have rights also – these are enshrined in law and practice (HM Government, 1995, 2000) (although they too were hard won) and these must be balanced with those of the disabled service user.

Certainly it is ironic that health and safety statutes prevent paid care workers from working in some situations, yet carers consistently work in these conditions. It is unwise and inhumane to fail to acknowledge the effects that unsafe working practices have on carers. Purely on economic terms, if a person is worn down by unrealistic and excessive levels of support work, they will certainly fail eventually, usually on health grounds themselves (Hirst, 1998). Thus, policy makers and professionals have at last begun to seriously acknowledge this situation, albeit that levels of input and support for carers are generally at such restricted levels that, at best, they shore up the carer, rather than realistically enable them to have an independent life away from caring, should they so choose.

Balancing disabled people's rights with those of an informal carer is a difficult task for a professional. Sometimes, in such situations, disabled people decline offers of replacement care because the replacement carers are inferior to the informal carer in their view. In other situations, disabled people have poor experiences in 'respite' care facilities or residential care homes and are unwilling to go again. This can leave the carer feeling they have no choice and that they cannot exercise their right to have a break from the work of caring. The role of the practitioner in such a situation is to stimulate discussion between all parties on the best way of producing a situation in which neither party is exploited or feels unsafe. It is also essential that the practitioner constantly strives to advocate on behalf of the dyad for higher quality replacement care which is minimally invasive, that may facilitate a way out of this vicious circle.

WHAT DO YOU THINK?

Imagine that you are about to visit a disabled man and his wife who is his carer. You already know that social services have been involved for a number of years with this dyad, but that now the carer is experiencing health problems and panic attacks. The disabled man has had a bad experience of a short break in a private residential care home and is refusing to go there again.

Think through the rights of both individuals separately.

How can these rights be balanced to produce a good outcome for both parties?

In situations where the rights of both a disabled person and carer must be balanced, relationships and contact with wider service providers are often critical. Social service practitioners have a pivotal role in facilitating access to other service providers who can assist and ameliorate in difficult situations of stress. In particular, the voluntary 'third' sector produces many services that are of use to disabled people and can provide assistance and support to carers also.

The national and local Centres for Integrated or Inclusive Living, in particular, offer assistance and information within a user-led system of service provision. These centres are particularly noted for their excellent advocacy and advice services, particularly in relation to the management of Direct Payments. Health professionals, particularly those working in domiciliary care, also have a critical role in highlighting stressed situations and offering preventive support or referral to other sources of assistance.

In deteriorating situations, where it is clearly difficult to make the distinction between the disabled person's and informal carer's rights, it is useful to utilise a framework in order to work out what outcomes each person is aiming to achieve and how they may be assisted in achieving them.

It is for this reason that the Outcomes for Disabled Service Users Framework was developed (Harris et al., 2005). The Framework has 26 domains. However, the uniqueness of the Outcomes approach is that it is led and driven by the disabled person rather than the professional and the latter's role is to create a record under the relevant domains, constantly checking that the manner of recording matches with the service user's intended outcome.

The stated outcomes for Disabled Service Users Framework (Harris et al., 2005: 52) are as follows:

- Personal care and comfort
- Access in/around the home
- Equipment/aids
- Transport
- Financial
- Transfers
- Physical health/wellbeing
- Domestic/activities daily living
- Mobility
- Communication
- Visual
- Cognitive
- Safety and security
- Housing/accommodation
- Carer issues
- Employment/education/training
- Social/leisure/recreation
- Information/advice
- Care package/hours
- Parenting and relationships
- Emotional wellbeing
- Independence
- Referral other professionals
- Legal
- Access community
- Citizenship.

In the above project (Harris et al., 2005), professionals found that in situations where disabled people voiced long-term outcomes, it was important to have stepping stones of 'smaller outcomes' that got the process going and facilitated a positive sense of achievement. Thus for example, a person who has a desired outcome of becoming more involved in their local community who has never done this before, could have a final outcome of taking a job in a third sector organisation. This might necessitate discussion on the achievement of smaller outcomes, such as access courses at the local College, mentoring from a member of a disabled persons' group and preparations for qualifying examinations.

Often, outcomes and goals are not as large and may involve something as minor as being able to access the outside areas of the home or do some gardening. Ultimately, the size of the outcome does not matter. It is the change in professional orientation of practice that is critical, with the professional acting as facilitator to other sources of assistance and advice and (where their profession dictates) as a recorder of the progress made on each visit. The disabled person is not only directly involved in the production of their desired outcome, they are responsible for the pace of progress and in control of the developing situation.

At the time of its piloting and implementation (2005), professionals viewed the Framework as highly innovatory and, although some struggled with relinquishing 'expert power', the vast majority recognised that focusing on outcomes, rather than professionally-defined 'needs' was a critical and important step forward on the road to user-led service provision. Disabled people in the study area found the production process of their own outcomes challenging but rewarding, ultimately a great step forward from 'traditional' service modes.

Critically, the Outcomes Framework allows disabled service users to be 'seen' by professionals in their own context; the situation of their own life with various forms of personal assistance. By placing the orientation of the work in the hands of the service user, professionals are constantly reminded of the fact that all professional work has the ultimate aim of improving their situation *in the service user's intended direction*. Ultimately, whilst professionals still have a role in the lives of disabled people, their aim should be assistive and facilitative only.

Relating the legislation and policy to the practice environment: how can professionals develop 'real reflexivity' in working with disabled people?

In previous chapters we have seen how the NHS and Community Care Act (HM Government, 1990) proved to be a catalyst for a new way of thinking about the production of services, assistance and support to disabled people in the UK. Community care, despite shaky beginnings and a few crises, is now well established as the norm for the majority of disabled people. The follow-on legislation and successive policy documents have served to further two general intentions in the original Act.

Firstly, and most importantly, disabled people have gradually taken more and more control over the production of personal assistance and support services. Disabled people now also have far more choice concerning personal assistance and support services. It is hard to imagine now that only 10 years prior to writing this book, an individual disabled person could have been offered no choice between service types, or direct payment usage against utilising traditional social services.

Secondly, Every Child Matters (DfES, 2003) had the effect of splitting social service provision down the middle, with all children coming under the remit of Education, and services for 'vulnerable adults' coming under Health. This would include people with mental health problems, people with learning difficulties and people with 'profound, multiple' impairments. Historically, health services have always held more power and sway than social services and this Act is widely recognised as the final nail in the coffin of statutory social work involvement with disabled people. Whether this is a good thing for disabled people in contact with professionals, now from Health, is debatable and it remains to be seen whether disabled people receive better or worse service provision as a result of the changes.

Relating these changes to the practice environment, as we have seen above, heralded a sea-change in the provision of professional services. The original Community Care legislation made it plain that professionals should henceforth act as facilitators to other service providers, rather than provide services from within social services. However, policing this sea-change proved impossible for the most part and this good intention was largely lost, mainly owing to the ability of local politicians to protect posts through continuation of in-house services. Thus, the original Act was before its time in many respects, and had it been followed through to the letter and spirit, traditional social service provision could also have circumvented becoming a white elephant and largely redundant service, out of step with the realities of post-modern Britain.

There are many disabled people in the UK who are very disenchanted with traditional professional services, particularly social service provision, which has been classified as stigmatising and paternalistic. There are those also, who see the detachment of adult social care for disabled people from social services (in England and Wales), or at least its move into Health, as the death throes of a failed service, focused too much on professional expert power at the expense of those who are on the receiving end.

Moves towards self-assessment, which cannot come too soon for many disabled people, are viewed in a similar light, as is the trend towards the inclusion of more groups of people in receipt of Direct Payments and Individual Budgets. All these innovations move power away from professionals and place it firmly in the hands of disabled people. As such these are welcome moves for those disabled people who can avail themselves of these innovations. However, it is likely that there will always be a core group of disabled people who cannot or do not wish to organise or participate in their own care provision. Disabled people in this core group and professionals who work with them, could benefit by using the Outcomes for Disabled People Framework, as described above.

Conclusion

In this chapter we examined key challenges for an aspiring practitioner wishing to use the social model of disability as a basis for positive practice. We have looked at the challenge of user control and choice and ways of approaching these issues for social model practitioners. 'Managing the Managers' is a difficult issue in the production of service to disabled people. Budgetary constraints and street-level bureaucracy can be major stumbling blocks to positive practice and many practitioners must learn to work within a disempowering system.

We have explored the difficult issues of 'mental capacity' and 'Power of Attorney', and seen how the social worker's duty of care can be balanced with social model practice, although this again is a complicated issue and, in practice, balancing skills must be developed over time. The many benefits of working with colleagues in user-led organisations such as modelling practice and learning have been explored and we have considered how professionals can develop 'real reflexivity' in working with disabled people. Reflexive practice is a skill that takes time to develop. Practitioners can utilise the Outcomes Framework to ensure that their practice is steered and directed by the disabled person and that they keep to their role in the process of facilitating the desired outcome.

Further reading

DoH (2005a) *Independence Wellbeing and Choice: Our Vision for the Future of Social Care for Adults in England*. London: Department of Health.

Harris J. (2004) 'Incorporating the Social Model into Outcome-Focused Social Care Practice with Disabled People', in C. Barnes and G. Mercer (eds) *Implementing the Social Model of Disability: Theory and Research*. Leeds: Disability Press.

SCIE (2008) *Co-Production: An Emerging Evidence Base for Adult Social Care Transformation, SCIE Research Briefing 31*. Available at: http://www.scie.org.uk/publications/briefings/briefing31/index.asp (accessed 19/10/09).

9

Conclusion

In this book we have portrayed the journey that disability policy has undergone over successive years, following key enactments of legislation. In tracing these changes, it is apparent that the world for disabled people is very different now than it was in 1900 or 1800. Many of the reforms that have taken place owe their existence to philanthropic endeavours based squarely on the simple humanitarian wish to improve disabled people's lives. However, it is only in very recent times that disabled people themselves have shaped the types of service they wish to use and this has resulted in a sea-change in the relationship that disabled people have with professionals. As documented above, successive legislation and policy in the modern era created the fertile conditions for disabled people's direct action in this respect and we are now entering an exciting stage where disabled people shape disability policy, rather than merely live with the consequences of non-disabled policy making.

In many respects, the changes that have resulted in disabled people becoming shapers of policy were born from intense dissatisfaction with the status quo. The social model of disability (Oliver, 1990) was one such watershed born out of a reaction to paternalistic (social) service provision that took little or no account of individual choice, and did not allow for user control. Thus, the services latterly and currently developed by disabled people's organisations, such as those in the Centres for Independent/Inclusive Living are uniquely positioned to promote not just these services, but also the underlying philosophy of the social model of disability upon which they are based.

Where do professionals from the Health and Social Services fit in this brave new world? Indeed, we could ask, is there a place for professionals from these professions in the new world of user-led services, personalisation and self-assessment? The answers to these questions really depend critically on whether the professionals in question are prepared to abandon their claims to expert power and embrace a role as facilitator; to move away from direction and embrace assistance. This is going to be the acid test that ultimately will demonstrate whether or not there is any worth in the retention of old style services. For social work in particular, it really is 'change or die'. Positive practitioners who wish to embrace their new roles can learn much from colleagues in user-led organisations, in particular, the practical application of the tenets of the social model of disability. Organisations like In Control are poised as the next generation of new style service provision.

In order to work effectively as a facilitator to other services and to provide desired assistance, practitioners will need to use different principles and modes of working that are based on the social model of disability, such as the Outcomes Framework described in the previous chapter. Crucially, disabled people both individually and collectively wish to control and choose the types of assistance they want. If professionals are to have a role in the future, it is in meeting these personalised and desired outcomes and facilitating access to other bodies who can meet them.

Given the policy background and the history described in this book, could there ever be such a thing as a 'social model practitioner' or is this an oxymoron? There are those who would think it is. However, it is likely that a considerable proportion of disabled people would wish to have access to assistance and advice from Health and Social Service professionals, provided this could be given within a framework that acknowledges the primacy and importance of their desired outcomes and that seeks to empower rather than disempower them.

As we have seen, the motivation of disabled people has been to successively gain more independence, choice and control over services. The Independent Living movement has been pivotal in providing a philosophy as well as a practical framework within which disabled people can orient their lives. Crucially, the movement away from services provided within a concessionary framework to one based on rights, was a critical moment in the development of disability policy. As we have seen, rights to services or amounts of money for services, more than anything else, foster independence and user choice and control.

Whilst we have drawn broad parallels across all disabled people to address our title, it is vital that we do not lose sight of the diversity of disability oppression, impairment effects and interface with chronic health conditions that form the bedrock of disabled people's experiences. Added to these statuses, we must consider race and ethnicity, gender and sexuality issues, as well as those related to age and age-appropriateness. All people are different from one another as well as having some similarities and common interests and the way that the differences interface with policy is often a critical determinant of their success or failure. In many ways, the success of a policy can be determined by the breadth of its applicability across these differences and the extent to which it can accommodate them and stimulate the production of empowering practices.

Services for disabled people have undergone a radical shift in recent times. Many will argue that it has not been radical enough and that there are still too many instances of disempowering practice occurring. The social model of disability has inspired many disabled people to move into the provision of their own services, through individual budgets or direct payments, or through engagement within user-led organisations. Whilst the latter do not make up a substantial amount of the overall service provision to disabled people as yet (in relation to the size of traditional statutory services), their influence and size grows daily and their popularity with disabled people is undoubted. At the heart of this matter lies the simple truth that no disabled people want to experience disempowering or paternalistic services, which is why they are not designed that way. User-led organisations score highly because they give and do not erode, users' choice and control. A practitioner implementing a social model framework will respect this critical distinction and seek to bolster and assist disabled people's choices, rather than continue to subscribe to outdated notions of 'expert power'.

The growth of managers and management within Health and Social Service organisations has presented disabled people with issues concerning levels of bureaucracy that have proved frustrating to say the least. 'Assessment' processes that are time-consuming and laborious, and that also reinforce feelings of disempowerment have contributed substantially to frustration levels. Underlying these issues however, one can see that these are matters of gloss on a strictly hierarchical system, which does not take account of user power, choices or rights. However, there is no prima facie reason why this system should operate in this way, and we have attempted to show examples of empowering systems in this book. Budgetary constraints arise in all public services and are a fact of life. There is never an easy way to deal with services that are required but cannot be afforded, but a system based on equitable provision and transparency of process at least gives users access to the basis upon which the decisions have been made.

In situations where 'mental capacity' is under debate, the issue of balancing the professional duty of 'care' with social model practice can be acute. There are no straightforward solutions or formulae that can be applied as each situation presents unique challenges. However, the motivation to act from the least position of power possible and correct utilisation of advocates and facilitators, can tip the balance in favour of the user.

'Expert power' is a core issue that has dogged traditional Health and Social Service provision and which has resulted in more than just inappropriate structures and mountains of bureaucracy. If we are to go forward and design empowering services that disabled people want to use we could do a lot worse than examine the models provided by the user-led organisations run by disabled people. What is required is a system within which disabled people have equality of access to assist them to achieve their desired outcomes, whatever these are. A social model practitioner seeks to act as a facilitator first and foremost, and as an assistant in the process of the achievement of the desired outcome. The disabled person takes, or should take central stage. Professionals may have to consider how to balance the disabled person's rights with those of any informal carers. This is another issue where there are no right answers and the practitioner must tread a careful path using some of the guidance we suggest.

If you are an aspiring social model practitioner, or just a professional interested in positive practice, how can you put the lessons in this book into practice? Firstly, and most importantly, learn more about disabled people's user-led organisations and explore ways of working creatively with disabled people in their organisations in order to produce better service outcomes for all disabled people. Model your practice on that of colleagues in user-led organisations and you will not go far wrong. Expose your colleagues to lessons you learn in interacting in these organisations.

Secondly, engage in real reflexive practice – consider seriously your value base, why you do your job and what you really want to achieve for the disabled people you serve. Use some of the exercises in this book with colleagues and compare notes on your answers. Keep in mind the principles of user choice and control and the centrality of the user's desired outcome. Learn more about how to become a good facilitator and assistant in the production of the desired outcome. Remember that personalisation is more than a policy directive; it should be about the design and achievement of the service user's desired outcomes.

Thirdly, ensure that you really understand the social model of disability and the meaning that it holds for all disabled people. Practice based on the social model of disability seeks to recognise the oppression meted out by non-disabled people and to counter this with positive practice at every opportunity. This involves reflexivity to ensure motivations are in line with the social model, advocacy where appropriate and empowerment of service users in striving to achieve the desired outcomes.

Finally, consider the merit of adopting positive practice based on the Outcomes Framework. Remember at all times the centrality of the disabled person's view; the importance of acting as a facilitator to other sources of assistance and the central importance of the service user's choice and control at all times.

Bibliography

Abberley, P. (1987) 'The Concept of Oppression and the Development of a Social Theory of Disability', *Disability, Handicap and Society*, 2(1): 5–19.

Adams, F. (1986) *Special Education*. London: FT and Prentice Hall.

Adams, R. and Campling, J. (1998) *Quality Social Work*. London, Palgrave Macmillan.

Adams, R., Dominelli, L. and Payne, M. (2002) *Social Work: Themes, Issues and Critical Debates*. Basingstoke: Macmillan.

Adams, R., Dominelli, L. and Payne, M. (eds) (2009) *Practising Social Work in a Complex World*. Basingstoke: Palgrave.

Age Concern and Help the Aged (2009) *Prevention in Practice: Service Models, Method and Impact*. London: Age Concern and Help the Aged.

Aldgate, J., Healey, L., Malcolm, B., Pine, P., Rose, W. and Seden, J. (eds) (2007) *Enhancing Social Work Management: Theory and Best Practice from the UK and USA*. London: Jessica Kingsley.

Ali, N., Atkin, K., Craig, G., Dadze-Arthur, A., Elliott, E. and Edwards, A. (2006) Ethnicity, Disability and Work. Examining the Inclusion of People with Sensory Impairments from Black and Minority Ethnic Groups into the Labour Market. Social Research Papers, Social Policy. Hull: University of Hull.

Arksey, H., O'Malley, L., Baldwin, S., Harris, J., Mason, A. and Golder, S. (2002) *Literature Review Report: Services to Support Carers of People with Mental Health Problems*. London: University of York and NCCSDO. Available at: http://www.sdo.nihr.ac.uk/files/adhoc/15-briefing-paper.pdf (accessed 19/10/09).

Aspire (2007) *Aspire Annual Report*. Stanmore: Aspire Publications.

Baker-Shenk, C. and Kyle, J. (1990) 'Research with Deaf People: Issues and Conflicts', *Disability, Handicap and Society*, 5(1): 65–75.

Bamford, C., Vernon, A., Nicholas, E. and Qureshi, H. (1999) *Outcomes of Social Care for Disabled People and their Carers*. Outcomes in Community Care Practice, Number Six. York: Social Policy Research Unit, University of York.

Barnes, C. (1990) *Cabbage Syndrome: The Social Construction of Dependency*. Falmer: London.

Barnes, C. (1991) *Disabled People in Britain and Discrimination: A Case for Anti Discrimination Legislation*. London: Hurst and BCODP.

Barnes, C. (1997) *Older Peoples' Perceptions of Direct Payments and Self Operated Support Systems*. Derby: BCODP and Help the Aged.

Barnes, C. and Mercer, G. (eds) (2004) *Implementing the Social Model of Disability: Theory and Research*. Leeds: Disability Press.

Barnes, C. and Mercer, G. (2007) *Independent Futures: Creating User-led Disability Services in a Disabling Society*. Bristol: Policy Press.

Barton, L. (2001) (ed.) *Disability Politics and the Struggle for Change*. London: David Fulton.

Barton, L. and Armstrong, F. (2007) *Policy, Experience and Change: Cross Cultural Reflections on Inclusive Education*. Dordrecht: Springer.

Bates, P. (2007) 'Safe and Sound', *Mental Health Today*, Feb, p. 32-34.

Bates, P. (2008) 'Socially Inclusive Practice', in T. Stickley, P. Lindley and T. Basset (eds) (2008) *Learning about Mental Health Practice*. Chichester: John Wiley & Sons.

Bauer, M., Fitzgerald, L., Haesler, E. and Manfrin, M. (2009) 'Hospital Discharge Planning for Frail Older People and their Family: Are We Delivering Best Practice? A Review of the Evidence', *Journal of Clinical Nursing*, 18(18): 2539–46.

BBC (2007) 'Carers Save the UK £87bn a year'. Available at: http://news.bbc.co.uk/1/hi/health/7001160.stm (accessed 19/10/09).

BCODP (1987) *Summary on the Report of the Audit Commission*. London: British Council of Organisations of Disabled People.

Beresford, B. and Oldman, C. (2002) *Housing Matters*. Bristol: Policy Press.

Beresford, P. and Harding, T. (1993) *A Challenge to Change: Practical Experiences of Building User Led Services*. London: NISW.

BGS (British Geriatrics Society) (2008) *Intermediate Care: Guidance for Commissioners and Providers of Health and Social Care*. London: BGS.

Bichard Inquiry Report HC653. London: The Stationery Office.

Binet, A. and Simon, T. (1916) *The Development of Intelligence in Children*. Baltimore: Williams & Wilkins.

Blair, T. (1997) 'Welfare Reform: Giving People the Will to Win', speech, Southwark, England, 2 June 1997.

BMA (2004) *Assessment of the Mental Capacity Act: Guidance for Doctors and Lawyers*. London: BMA.

BMA and Law Society (2007) *Mental Capacity Tool Kit*. London: BMA/Law Society.

Bonnett, D. (1996) *Incorporating Lifetime Homes Standards into Modernisation Programmes, Findings, Housing Research 174*. York: Joseph Rowntree Foundation.

Booth, T (2000) 'Parents with Learning Difficulties, Child Protection and the Courts', *Representing Children*, 13(3): 175-188.

Bornat, J., Pereira, C., Pilgrim, D. and Williams, F. (eds) (1993) *Community Care: A Reader*. Basingstoke: Macmillan.

Borsay, A. (2005) *Disability and Social Policy in Britain since 1750: A History of Exclusion*. Basingstoke: Palgrave.

Bramwell R., Harrington F. and Harris, J. (2000a) 'Deaf Women: Informed Choice, Policy and Legislation', *British Journal of Midwifery*, 8(9): 545–8.

Bramwell, R., Harrington F. and Harris, J. (2000b) 'Deafness – Disability or Linguistic Minority?', *British Journal of Midwifery*, 8(4): 222–24.

Bramwell R., Harrington F. and Harris, J. (2002) 'Deaf Women: Informed Choice, Policy and Legislation', in F.J. Harrington and G.H. Turner (2002) *Interpreting: Studies and Reflections on Sign Language Interpreting*. Coleford: Douglas McLean.

Brandon, D., Hawkes, A. (1998) *Speaking Truth to Power: Care Planning for People with Disabilities*. London: Venture Press.

Braye, S. and Preston-Shoot, M. (1993) 'Partnership: Responding to the Challenge, Realising the Potential', *Social Work Education*, 12(2): 35–53.

Brayne, H. and Martin, G. (1999) *Law for Social Workers*, 6th edn. London: Blackstone.

Brechin, A., Liddiard, P. and Swain, J. (1981) (eds) *Handicap in a Social World*. Sevenoaks: Hodder and Stoughton.

Brewster, J. and Ramcharan, P. (2005) 'Enabling and Supporting Person-Centred Approaches', in Grant, G., Goward, P., Richardson, M. and Ramcharan, P. (eds) *Learning Disability: A Life Cycle Approach to Valuing People*. Maidenhead: Open University Press.

Brisenden, S. (1986) 'Independent Living and the Medical Model of Disability', *Disability, Handicap and Society*, 1(2): 173–8.

Bulletin of Royal College of Psychiatrists (1989) London: Royal College of Psychiatrists.

Campbell, J. (2003) 'Putting what Service Users Say into Policy and Practice', plenary speech to Improving Quality, Increasing Involvement: Making it Real SOLNUN Conference, London 25 June.

Campbell, J. and Oliver, M. (1996) *Disability Politics: Understanding Our Past, Changing Our Future*. London: Routledge.

Chadwick, R. and Russell, J. (1989) 'Hospital Discharge of Frail Elderly People: Social and Ethical Considerations in the Discharge Decision-making Process', *Ageing and Society*, 9: 277–95.

Clarke, J., Gewirtz, S. and McLaughlin, E. (2000) *New Managerialism, New Welfare*. London: Sage.

Cobbold, C. (1997) *A Cost Benefit Analysis of Lifetime Homes*. York: Joseph Rowntree Foundation.

Contact a Family (2006) *Wheelchair Services for Children and Young People in Wales*. Cardiff: Contact a Family Wales.

Cooper, J. (2000) *Law, Rights and Disability*. London: Jessica Kingsley.

Crichton, J (1998) 'The Bournewood Judgment and Mental Incapacity', *Journal of Forensic Psychiatry and Psychology*, 9 (3): 513–17.

CSIE (2004) *Inclusive Education: Readings and Reflections*. London: Centre for Studies in Inclusive Education & McGraw Hill Education.

Davey, V., Fernández, J-L., Knapp, M., Vick, N., Jolly, D., Swift, P., Tobin, R., Kendall, J., Ferrie, J., Pearson, C., Mercer, G. and Priestley, M. (2006) *Direct Payments Survey: A National Survey of Direct Payments Policy and Practice*, Personal Social Services Research Unit/London School of Economics and Political Science.

Davis, K. (1998) *The Disabled Peoples' Movement: Putting the Power in Empowerment*. Available at: http://www.leeds.ac.uk/disability-studies/archiveuk/DavisK/davis-empowerment.pdf (accessed 10/8/09).

Daw, R. (2003) *The Impact of the Human Rights Act on Disabled People*. London: Disability Rights Commission.

Deegan, M.J. (1981) 'Multiple Minority Groups: A Case Study of Physically Disabled Women', *Journal of Sociology & Social Welfare*, 8(2): 247–95.

Digby, A. (1985) *Madness, Morality and Medicine: A Study of the York Retreat, 1796–1914*. Cambridge: Cambridge University Press.

Disability Concern Glasgow (2007) *Better Health, Better Care: A Discussion Document*. Available at http://www.scotland.gov.uk/Resource/Doc/211243/0056079.pdf (accessed 10/08/09).

Disabled Parents Network (2005) 'Housing' section of *Disabled Parents Information Briefing on Services*, Disabled Parents Network. See publication details on: www.DisabledParents Network.org.uk

Drake, R. (1999) *Understanding Disability Policies*. Basingstoke: Macmillan.

Driedger, D. (1989) *The Last Civil Rights Movement*. London: Hurst.

Duffy, S. (2008) 'Personalised Care: Disabled People Taking Charge of their Lives', *Community Care*, 21 January.

EDCM (2009) *Disabled Children's Manifesto for Change*. Available at: http://www.edcm.org. uk/dcmanifesto/dc_manifesto.pdf (accessed 19/10/09).

Emerson, E. (1990) 'Designing Individualised Community Based Placements as an Alternation to Institutions for People with Severe Mental Handicap and Severe Problem Behaviour', in W.I. Fraser, *Key Issues in Mental Retardation Research*. Abingdon: Routledge. pp. 395–404.

Emerson, E. (2001) *Challenging Behaviour: Analysis and Intervention in People with Severe Intellectual Disabilities*. Cambridge: Cambridge University Press.

Emerson, E. (2005) 'Models of Service Delivery', in G. Grant, P. Goward, M. Richardson and P. Ramcharan (eds) *Learning Disability: A Life Cycle Approach to Valuing People*. Buckingham: Open University Press.

Erwin-Jones, S. (2008) 'Choose your Partners', *Community Care*, 5 June.

Fenton, M. and Hughes, P. (1993) *Passivity to Empowerment: A Living Skills Curriculum for People with Disabilities*. London: RADAR.

Finch J. (1984), 'Community Care: Developing Non-sexist Alternatives', *Critical Social Policy*, (10): 6-18.

Finch, J. and Groves, D. (1983) *A Labour of Love*. London: RKP.

Finkelstein, V. (1980) *Attitudes and Disabled People: Issues for Discussion*. New York: World Rehabilitation Monograph.

Finkelstein, V (1993) 'The Commonality of Disability', in J. Swain, V. Finkelstein, S. French and M. Oliver, (1993) *Disabling Barriers, Enabling Environments*. London, Sage.

Foster, M., Harris, J., Jackson, K. and Glendinning, C. (2006a) 'Practitioners' Documentation of Assessment and Care Planning in Social Care – the Opportunities for Organizational Learning', *British Journal of Social Work*. Available at: http://bjsw.oxfordjournals.org/cgi/reprint/bcl366?

Foster, M., Harris, J., Jackson, K. and Morgan, H. (2006b) 'Personalised Social Care for Adults with Disabilities: A Problematic Concept for Frontline Practice. *Health and Social Care in the Community*, 14(2): 125–35.

Foucault,, M. (1961) *Madness and Civilization: A History of Insanity in the Age of Reason*. Paris: Librarie Plan.

Foucault, M. (1977) *Discipline and Punish: The Birth of the Prison*. New York: Pantheon.

Foucault, M. (2001) *Madness and Civilisation*. London: Routledge.

Fraser, D. (2002) *The Evolution of the British Welfare State*. Basingstoke: Palgrave.

French, S (1994) *On Equal Terms: Working with Disabled People*. London: Butterworth-Heinemann.

Fulcher, G. (1989) *Disabling Policies? A Comparative Approach to Educational Policy and Disability*. Lewes: Falmer.

Glasby, J. and Littlechild, R. (2002) (eds) *Social Work and Direct Payments*. Bristol: Policy Press.

Gleeson, B. (1999) *Geographies of Disability*. London: Routledge.

Glendinning, C. and Kemp, P.A. (eds) (2006) *Cash and Care: Policy Challenges in the Welfare State*. Bristol: Policy.

Glendinning, C., N, Moran., Rabiee, P., Challid, D., Jacobs, S., Wilberforce, M., Knapp, M., Fernandez, J.L., Netten, A. and Jones, K. (2008) *The IBSEN project - National evaluation of the Individual Budgets Pilot Projects*. London: Department of Health. Available at (IBSEN) www.dhcarenetworks.org.uk/

Goffman, E. (1961) *Asylums: Essays on the Social Situation of Mental Patients*. New York: Anchor Doubleday.

Gooding, C. (1996) *Disabling Policies, Enabling Acts*. London: Pluto.

Government Actuary's Department (2003) *National Statistics: Expectation of Life at Birth*. London: GAD.

Grant, G., Goward, P., Richardson, M. and Ramcharan, P. (eds) (2005) *Learning Disability: A Life Cycle Approach to Valuing People*. Maidenhead: Open University Press.

Green-Hernandez, C., Singleton, J.K. and Aronzon, D.Z. (2001) (eds) *Primary Care Paediatrics*. Philadelphia: Lippincott Williams and Wilkins.

Griffiths Report (1988) *Community Care: An Agenda for Action*. London: HMSO.

Harris, J. (1995a) *The Cultural Meaning of Deafness: Language, Identity & Power Relations*. Aldershot, Hants: Avebury Publications.

Harris, J. (1995b) 'Boiled Eggs & Baked Beans: A Personal Account of a Hearing Researcher's Journey through Deaf Culture', *Disability & Society*, 10(3): 295–308.

Harris, J. (1997) *Deafness and the Hearing*. Birmingham: Venture Press.

Harris, J. (2003) '"All Doors are Closed to Us": A Social Model Analysis of the Experiences of Disabled Refugees and Asylum Seekers in Britain', *Disability & Society*, 18(4): 393–408.

Harris, J. (2004) 'Incorporating the Social Model into Outcome-Focused Social Care Practice with Disabled People', in C. Barnes and G. Mercer (eds) *Implementing the Social Model of Disability: Theory and Research*. Leeds: Disability Press.

Harris, J. and Bamford, C. (2001) 'The Uphill Struggle: Services for Deaf and Hard of Hearing People; Issues of Equality, Participation and Access', *Disability & Society*, 16(7): 969–80.

Harris, J. and Christie, A. (1992) 'Black Deaf People: Issues in Service Provision', *Deafness*, 9(2): 4–7.

Harris, J. and Huntington, A. (2000) 'Emotions as Analytical Tools: Parallels between Fieldwork and Psychodynamic Therapy', in K. Gilbert, *The Emotional Response*. Florida: CRC Press. 129–46.

Harris, J. and Morgan, H. (2002) *Outcomes for Disabled Service Users Interim Project Report*. SPRU, University of York/Department of Health, DH1924.11.02JH/HM.

Harris, J. and Paylor, I. (1999) 'The Politics of Difference', in B. Broad (ed.) *The Politics of Research and Evaluation in Social Work*. Birmingham: Venture Press. pp. 31–43.

Harris, J. and Roberts, K. (2003) 'Challenging Barriers to Participation in Qualitative Research: Involving Disabled Refugees', *International Journal of Qualitative Methods*, 2(2): Article 2. Retrieved 24 June 2003 from http://www.ualberta.ca/~iiqm/backissues/2_2/pdf/harrisetal.pdf

Harris, J. and Roberts, K. (2004) 'Not Our Problem: The Provision of Services to Disabled Refugees and Asylum Seekers', in D. Hayes and B. Humphries (eds) *Social Work, Immigration and Asylum: Debates, Dilemmas and Ethical Issues for Social Work and Social Care Practice*. London: Jessica Kingsley.

Harris, J. and Roberts, K. (2006) 'Challenging Barriers to Participation in Qualitative Research: Involving Disabled Refugees', in B. Temple and R. Moran (eds) *Doing Research with Refugees: Issues and Guidelines*. Bristol: The Policy Press. pp. 155–66.

Harris, J. and Stewart, J. (2000) 'Disability, Dependency and the Role of the Professional', in I. Paylor, L. Froggett and J. Harris (eds) (2000) *Reclaiming Social Work: The Southport Papers Volume 2*. Birmingham: Venture Press/BASW. pp. 85–98.

Harris, J. and Thornton, P. (2005) 'Deaf People and Employment', in A. Roulstone and C. Barnes (eds) *Working Futures: Disabled People, Policy and Social Inclusion*. Bristol: The Policy Press. pp. 233–45.

Harris, J., Arnott, J., Hine, N. and Kroll, T. (2009) *The Use, Role and Application of Advanced Technology in the Lives of Disabled People*. Final report to the Economic and Social Research

Council, UK. Available at: http://www.idris.ac.uk/book/Advance%20Tec/Project%20 Report%20FINAL%20copy%20for%20website.doc

Harris, J., Foster, M., Jackson, K. and Morgan, H. (2005) *Outcomes for Disabled Service Users*. Social Policy Research Unit, University of York. Available at: http://www.york.ac.uk/inst/ spru/pubs/pdf/service.pdf

Harris, J., Froggett, L. and Paylor, I. (eds) (2000) *Reclaiming Social Work: The Southport Papers, Volume I*. Birmingham, BASW/Venture Press.

Harris, J., Piper, S. and Morgan, H. (2008) 'Evidence from the National Service Framework for Long-Term Conditions. Abstracts from the Innovation in Rehabilitation: Applying Theory to Practice Conference, Rotorua, New Zealand 16–17 February 2007', *Disability and Rehabilitation*, 29(20–1): 1634–63.

Harris, J., Piper, S., Morgan, H., Thomas, C., McClimmens, A., Shah, S., Barnes, C., Mercer, G., Arksey, H. and Qureshi, H. (2003a) *Brief Review Study: National Service Framework for Long Term Conditions, 'User's Experiences of Health and Social Care Services'*. SPRU, University of York, DH 1966 JH0403.

Harris, J., Piper, S., Morgan, H., McClimmens, A., Shah, S., Reynolds, H., Baldwin, S., Arksey, H. and Qureshi, H. (2003b) *Brief Review Study: National Service Framework for Long Term Conditions, 'Carer's experiences of Providing Care for People with a Long Term Condition'*. SPRU, University of York. DH 1968 JH0703.

Harris, J., Sapey, B. and Stewart, J. (1997a) 'Estimating Disabled Needs Locally', *Housing Review*, 46(6): 127–9.

Harris, J., Sapey, B. and Stewart, J. (1997b) *Wheelchair Housing and the Estimation of Need*, commissioned by the National Wheelchair Housing Association Group.

Harris, J., Sapey, B. and Stewart, J. (2000) 'Blairfare: Third Way Disability and Dependency in Britain', *Disability Studies Quarterly*, 19(4): 360–71.

Henwood, M. and Hudson, B. (2007) *Here to Stay? Self-Directed Support: Aspiration and Implementation*. Towcester: Melanie Henwood Associates. Report Commissioned by the Department of Health.

Henwood, F. and Turner, L. (2007) *Better Outcomes, Lower Costs: Implications for Health and Social Care Budgets of Investment in Housing Adaptations, Improvements and Equipment. A Review of the Evidence*. Leeds: Department for Work and Pensions.

Hirsch, D. (2006) *Paying for Long Term Care: Moving Forwards*. York: Joseph Rowntree Foundation.

Hirst, M. (1998) *The Health of Informal Carers: A Longitudinal Analysis*. Working Paper 1563, Social Policy Research Unit, University of York.

Holman, A. and Collins, J. (1997) *Funding Freedom: A Guide to Direct Payments for People with Learning Difficulties*. London: Values into Action.

Humphries, S and Gordon, P (1992) *Out of Sight: The Experience of Disability 1900-1950*. Plymouth : Northcote House,

Hyde, M. (1998) 'Sheltered and Supported Employment in the 1990s: The Experiences of Disabled Workers in the UK', *Disability & Society*, 13(2): 199–215.

Ibsen Consortium (2007) *Individual Budgets Evaluation: A Summary of Early Findings*. Study for the Department of Health. Available at: www.ibsen.org.uk

Jack, R. (ed.) (1993) *Empowerment in Community Care*. London: Chapman Hall.

Johnson, T.J. (1977) *Professions and Power*. London: Heinemann.

Jones, C. and Novak, T. (1999) *Poverty, Welfare and the Disciplinary State*, London: Routledge.

Jones, S. and Morgan, J. (2002) Making it Work: Success in Supported Employment for People with Learning Difficulties. York: Joseph Rowntree Foundation.

King's Fund (2009) *Funding Adult Social Care in England*. London: King's Fund.

King's Fund and National Development Team (1996) *Changing Days: Developing New Opportunities with People who have Learning Difficulties*. London: King's Fund and NDT.

King's Fund Centre (1980) *An Ordinary Life*. London: King's Find.

Kroll, T., Barbour, R. and Harris, J. (2007) 'Using Focus Groups in Disability Research', *Qualitative Health Research*, 7(5): 690–8.

Kyle, J.G. and Baker-Shenk, C. (1990) 'Research with Deaf People: Issues and Conflicts', *Disability, Handicap and Society*, 5(1): 65–75.

Lakey, J. (1994) *Caring About Independence: Disabled People and the Independent Living Fund*. London: Policy Studies Institute.

Laming, W.H. (2003) (Climbié Enquiry Report) *The Victoria Climbié Enquiry: Summary and Recommendations*. TSO, Norwich.

Lane, H. (1989) *When the Mind Hears: A History of the Deaf*. New York: Random House.

Lane, H.L. (2002) 'Do Deaf People Have a Disability?', *Sign Language Studies*, 2(4): 356–79.

Lansley, P. (2001) 'The Promise and Challenge of Providing Assistive Technology to Older People', *Age and Ageing*, 30: 439–44.

Lawson, A. (2008) *Disability and Equality Law in Britain: The Role of Reasonable Adjustments*. Oxford: Hart Publishing.

Leece, J. and Bornat, J. (2006) *Developments in Direct Payments*. Bristol: Policy Press.

Lipsky, M. (1980) *Street-Level Bureaucracy: Dilemmas of the Individual in Public Services*. New York: Russell Sage Foundation.

LGA and ADSS (2006) *£1.77 Billion Social Care Shortfall Forces Difficult Decisions*. Local Government Association and Association of Directors of Social Services. Available at: http://www.lga.gov.uk/lga/core/page.do?pageId=45452 (accessed 19/10/09).

Lowe, R. (2005) *The Welfare State in Britain Since 1945*. Basingstoke: Macmillan.

Mair, R. (2009) 'Trying to Get it Right with Campus Closure', *Learning Disability Today*, August/September, 11.

Mansell, J., Knapp, M., Beadle-Brown, J. and Beecham, J. (2007) *Deinstitutionalisation and Community Living – Outcomes and Costs: Report of a European Study. Volume 1: Executive Summary*. Canterbury: Tizard Centre.

Martin, J., White, A. and Meltzer, H. (1989) *OPCS Surveys of Disability in Great Britain. Report 4: Disabled Adults, Services, Transport and Education*. London: HMSO.

Matson, N. (1994) 'Coping, Caring and Stress: A Study of Stroke Carers and Carers of Older Confused People', *British Journal of Clinical Psychology*, 33(3): 333–44.

McInnes, K. (2007) *A Practitioner's Guide to Interagency Working in Children's Centres: A Review of Literature*. Maidenhead: Barnardo's Policy and Research Unit.

Mead, N. and Bower, P. (2000) 'Patient-Centredness: A Conceptual Framework and Review of the Empirical Literature'. *Social Science and Medicine*, 55: 283–99.

Means, R. (2007) 'Safe as Houses? Ageing in Place and Vulnerable Older People in the UK', *Social Policy and Administration*, 41(1): 65–85.

Means, R., Richards, S. and Smith, R. (2008) *Community Care*, 4th edn. London: Palgrave.

Mencap (2007) *Death by Indifference*. London: Mencap.

Mickel, A. (2008) 'Personalisation: Exclusive Poll of Social Workers' Views', *Community Care*, October 2008. Available at: http://www.communitycare.co.uk/Articles/2008/10/22/109761/personalisation-exclusive-poll-of-social-workers-views.html (accessed 20/10/09).

Miller, E.J. and Gwynne,V.J. (1972) *A Life Apart*. London: Tavistock.

Minister of Health (1961) Address to the National Association of Mental Health Annual Conference, '*Water Tower*' Speech, 9 March.

Morgan, H. and Harris, J. (2002) 'Shaping Our Lives/Social Policy Research Unit, Social Care Outcomes Seminar: Issues for Professionals and Service Users', DH190410.02 HM/JH.

Morgan, H. and Harris, J. (2005) 'Strategies for Involving Service Users in Outcomes Focused Research', in L. Lowe and I. Hulatt (eds) *Involving Service Users in Health and Social Care Research*. London: Taylor & Francis.

Morgan, H., Barnes, C. and Mercer, G. (2001) *Creating Independent Futures: An Evaluation of Services Led by Disabled People. Stage Two Report*. Leeds: Disability Press.

Morris, J. (1991) *Pride against Prejudice: Transforming Attitudes to Disability*. London: The Women's Press.

Morris, J. (1993) *Independent Lives: Community Care and Disabled People*. Basingstoke: Macmillan.

Morris, J. (1997) *Community Care: Working in Partnership with Service Users*. Birmingham: Venture Press.

Morris, J. (1999) 'Disabled children, the Children Act and Human Rights'. Talk given at 'Young and Powerful' Conference, organised by Disability North, 26 May. Available at: http://www.leeds.ac.uk/disabilitystudies/archiveuk/morris/Disabled%20children,%20 the%20Children%20Act%20and%20human%20rights.pdf

Morris, P. (1969) *Put Away: A Sociological Study of the Institutions for the Mentally Retarded*. London: Routledge and Kegan Paul.

National Council for Palliative Care (2007) The Mental Capacity Act in Practice: Guidance for End of Life Care. http://www.ncpc.org.uk/publications/pubs_list.html

NCIL (2006) *Review of Adult Social Care*. Available at www.ncil.org.uk

Newman, J. (2007) *Modernisation of Adult Social Care – What's Working*. London: Department of Health.

NISW (1982) *Social Workers, Their Role and Tasks* (The Barclay Report). London: Bedford Square Press

O'Brien, M. and Harris, J. (1999) 'Modernity and The Politics of Identity', in M. O'Brien, S. Penna and C. Hay (eds) *Modernity and Reflexivity: Identity and Environment in Giddens' Social Theory*. Essex, UK: Addison Wesley Longman Limited. pp. 139–55.

O'Bryan, A., Simons, K., Beyer, S. and Grove, B. (2000) *A Framework for Supported Employment*. Manchester: National Development Team.

OECD (1996) *Ageing in OECD Countries: A Critical Policy Challenge*. Paris: Organisation for Economic Cooperation and Development.

Ofcom (2007) *Signing on Television: Proposed Changes*. Available at: http://www.ofcom.org.uk/ consult/condocs/signing/signing.pdf (accessed 19/10/09).

Oldman, C. (2002) 'Later Life and the Social Model of Disability: A Comfortable Partnership?', *Ageing and Society*, 22(6): 791–806.

Oliver, M. (1983) *Social Work with Disabled People*. Basingstoke: Macmillan.

Oliver, M. (1990) *The Politics of Disablement*. Basingstoke: Macmillan.

Oliver, M. (ed.) (1993) *Social Work: Disabled People and Disabling Environments*. London: Jessica Kingsley.

Oliver, M. and Barnes, C. (1998) *Disabled People and Social Policy: From Exclusion to Inclusion*. Harlow: Longman.

Oliver, M. and Sapey, B. (1999) *Social Work with Disabled People*. 2nd edn. Basingstoke: Macmillan.

Olsen, R. and Clarke, H. (2002) *Parenting and Disability: Disabled Parents' Experiences of Raising Children*. Bristol: Policy Press.

Parsloe, P. and Stevenson, O. (1993) *Community Care and Empowerment*. York: Joseph Rowntree Foundation.

Paylor, I., Froggett, L. and Harris, J. (Eds) (2000) *Reclaiming Social Work: The Southport Papers, Volume II*. Birmingham: BASW/Venture Press.

Peck, S. (2009) 'Shaw Announces More Money for Access to Work', *Disability Now*, 6 July.

Phillipson, C. (1998) *Reconstructing Old Age: New Agendas in Social Theory and Practice*. London: Sage.

PMSU (2005) Improving the Life Chances of Disabled People. A Joint Report with Department of Work and Pensions, Department of Health, Department for Education and Skills, Office of the Deputy Prime Minister.

Prideaux, S., Roulstone, A., Harris, J. and Barnes, C. (2009) 'Disabled People and Self-Directed Support Schemes: Reconceptualising Work and Welfare in the 21st Century', *Disability and Society*, 24(5): 557–69.

Priestley, M. (1999) *Disability Politics and Community Care*. London: Jessica Kingsley.

Priestley, M. (2000) 'Adults Only: Disability, Social Policy and the Life Course', *Journal of Social Policy*, 29(3): 421–39.

Priestley, M. (2003) *Disability: A Life Course Approach*. Cambridge: Polity.

Qureshi, H., Bamford, C., Nicholas, E., Patmore, C. and Harris, J. (2000) *Outcomes in Social Care Practice: Developing an Outcomes Focus in Care Managements and User Surveys*. Department of Health Report: DH1738.

Renshaw, C. (2008) 'Do Self-Assessment and Self-Directed Support Undermine Traditional Social Work with Disabled People?', *Disability and Society*, 23(3): 283–86.

Riddell, S., Weedon, E., Fuller, M., Healey, M., Hurst, A., Kelly, K. and Piggott, L. (2006) 'Managerialism and Equalities: Tensions Within Widening Access Policy and Practice for Disabled Students in UK Universities', *Higher Education*, 54(4): 615–28.

Roberts, K. and Harris, J. (2001) *Disabled Refugees and Asylum Seekers in Britain: Numbers and Social Characteristics*. SPRU, University of York, NLCB1816.05.01KR/Jha.

Roberts, S., Heaver, C., Hill, K., Rennison, J., Stafford, B., Howat, N., Kelly, G., Krishnan, S., Tapp, P. and Thomas, A. (2004) *Disability in the Workplace: Employers' and Service Providers' Responses to the Disability Discrimination Act in 2003 and Preparation for 2004 Changes*. DWP Research Report 202, Leeds, CDS.

Roulstone, A. (1998) *Enabling Technology: Disabled People, Work and New Technology*. Milton Keynes: Open University Press.

Roulstone, A. (2002) 'Disabling Pasts, Enabling Futures? How Does the Changing Nature of Capitalism Impact on the Disabled Worker and Jobseeker?', *Disability & Society*, 17(6): 627–42.

Roulstone, A (2007) What Can Assistive Technology Offer Disabled Adults? Research into Practice for Adults Outlines No.5. Dartington, Ripfa,

Roulstone, A. and Barnes, C. (2005) (eds) *Working Futures? Disabled People, Policy and Social Inclusion*. Bristol: Policy Press.

Roulstone, A. and Hudson, V. (2007) 'Carer Participation in England, Wales and Northern Ireland', *Journal of Interprofessional Care*, 23(3): 303-313.

Roulstone, A. and Morgan, H. (2009) 'Neo-Liberal Individualism or Self-Directed Support: Are We All Speaking the Same Language on Modernising Adult Social Care?', *Social Policy and Society*, 8(3): 333–45.

Roulstone, A. and Thomas, P. (2009) *Hate Crime and Disabled People*. Equality and Human Rights Commission and Breakthrough UK, Manchester.

Roulstone, A., Price, J., Child, L. and Gradwell, L. (2003) *Thriving and Surviving at Work: Disabled Peoples' Employment Strategies*. York: Joseph Rowntree Foundation.

Royal College of Physicians and Institute of Physics and Engineering in Medicine (2004) *Specialist Equipment Services For Disabled People: The Need For Change*. London: RCP and IPEM.

RCLTC (Royal Commission on Long-Term Care) (1999) (Sutherland Report) *With Respect to Old Age: Long Term Care – Rights and Responsibilities: A Report by The Royal Commission on Long-Term Care*. London: TSO.

Rummery, K. (2002) *Disability, Citizenship and Community Care: A Case for Welfare Rights*. Aldershot: Ashgate Publishing.

Ryan, J and Thomas, F (1980) *The Politics of Mental Handicap*. London. Penguin Books.

Ryan, J. and Thomas, F. (1987) *The Politics of Mental Handicap*. London: Free Association Books.

Samuel, M. (2009) 'Minster Defends Second Set of "Individual Budget" Pilots', *Community Care*, June. Available at: http://www.communitycare.co.uk/Articles/2009/06/17/111850/minster-defends-second-set-of-individual-budget-pilots.html (accessed 19/10/09).

Sapey, B. (1995) 'Disabling Homes: A Study of the Housing Needs of Disabled People in Cornwall', *Disability & Society*, 10(1): pp. 71–85.

Sapey, B. and Hewitt, N. (1993) 'The Changing Context of Social Work Practice', in M. Oliver (ed.) *Social Work, Disabled People and Disabling Environments*. London: Jessica Kingsley.

Sapey, B. and Pearson, J. (2004) 'Do Disabled People Need Social Workers?', *Social Work and Social Sciences Review*, 11(3): 52–70.

Sapey, B., Harris, J. and Stewart, J. (2005) 'Housing: Choice is the Key', *Disability, Pregnancy & Parenthood International*, 51. Available at: http://www.dppi.org.uk/journal/51/research.html

Sapey, B., Stewart, J. and Donaldson, G. (2004) *The Social Implications of Increases in Wheelchair Use*, Lancaster, Lancaster University. www.lancs.ac.uk/fss/apsocsci/wheelchair/index.htm

Sapey, B., Stewart, J. and Harris, J. (2001a) 'Disability: Constructing Dependency through Social Policy', in C. Baxter (ed.) *Managing Diversity and Inequality in Health Care*. Edinburgh: Bailliere Tindall/ Royal College of Nursing. pp. 122–42.

Sapey, B., Stewart, J. and Harris, J. (2001b) 'Welfare Enactments and Disabled People', in C. Baxter (ed.) *Managing Diversity and Inequality in Health Care*. Edinburgh: Bailliere Tindall/ Royal College of Nursing. pp. 143–9.

Sawhney, I., Mukhopadhyay, A. and Karki, C. (2009) 'Mental Capacity Act 2005: Views and Experiences of Learning Disability Psychiatrists', *Psychiatrist*, 33: 234-236.

Scottish Government, (2009) Personalisation: A Shared Understanding Commissioning for Personalisation A Personalised Commissioning Approach to Support and Care Services. Edinburgh: Changing Lives Service Development Group.

Scull, A. (1979) *Museums of Madness: The Social Organisation of Insanity in Nineteenth Century Britain*. London: Allen Lane.

Seebohm, F. (1968) Report of the Committee on Local Authority and Allied Personal Social Services (the Seebohm Report). London: HMSO.

Shah, S. (2006) *Career Success of Disabled High Flyers*. London: Jessica Kingsley.

Shah, S. and Priestley, M. (2001) Better Services, Better Health – The Healthcare Experiences of Black and Minority Ethnic Disabled People. Centre for Disability Studies: University of Leeds.

Shakespeare, T. (2000) 'Disabled Sexuality: Toward Rights and Recognition Disabled Sexuality', *Sexuality and Disability*, 18(3): 159–66.

Shakespeare, T. and Watson, N. (2001) 'The Social Model of Disability: An Outdated Ideology? Exploring Theories and Expanding Methodologies', *Research in Social Science and Disability*, 2: 9–28.

Shakespeare, T., Gillespie-Sells, K. and Davies, D. (1996) *The Sexual Politics of Disability*. London: Cassell.

Shaping our Lives (2002) *From Outset to Outcome: Report of Four Development Projects on User Defined Outcomes*. London: National Institute for Social Work.

Shaping our Lives et al. (2003) *From Outset to Outcome – What People Think of the Social Care Services They Use*. Shaping Our Lives, National User Network, Black User Group, Ethnic Disabled Group Emerged, Footprints, Waltham Forest Black Mental Health Service User Group and Service Users' Action Forum.

Sloper, P. (2004) 'Facilitators and Barriers for Co-ordinated Multi-Agency Services', *Child Care, Health and Development*, 30(6): 571–80.

Staincliffe, S. (2003) 'Wheelchair Services and Providers: Discriminating Against Disabled People', *International Journal of Therapy and Rehabilitation*, 10(4): 151–9.

Stewart, J., Harris, J. and Sapey, B. (1998) 'Truth or Manipulation? The Politics of Government-Funded Disability Research', *Disability & Society*, 13(2): 297–300.

Stewart, J., Harris, J. and Sapey, B. (1999) 'Disability & Dependency: Origins and Futures of "Special Needs" Housing for Disabled People', *Disability & Society*, 14(1): 5–20.

Stiker, H.J (2000) *A History of Disability*. Michigan: University of Michigan Press.

Stone, D. (1984) *The Disabled State*. Philadelphia: Temple Press.

Stuart, O. (1992) 'Race and Disability: Just a Double Oppression?', *Disability & Society*, 77(2): 177–88.

Swain, J. and French, S. (2000) 'Towards an Affirmation Model of Disability', *Disability & Society*, 15(4): 569–82.

Swain, J., Finkelstein, V., French, S. and Oliver, M. (eds) (1993) *Disabling Barriers, Enabling Environments*. Buckingham: Open University Press and Sage.

Swain, J., French, S., Barnes, C. and Thomas, C. (eds) (2004) *Disabling Barriers, Enabling Environments*, 2nd edn. London: Sage.

Taylor, C. and White, S. (2006) *Knowledge and Reason in Social Care*. Birmingham: BASW.

Thomas, C. (1999) *Female Forms: Experiencing and Understanding Disability*. Buckingham: Open University Press.

Thomas, C. (2007) *Sociologies of Disability and Illness: Contested Ideas in Disability Studies and Medical Sociologies*. Basingstoke: Palgrave.

Thompson, I., Melia, K. and Boyd, K. (2000) *Nursing Ethics*. London: Churchill Livingstone.

Thompson, N. (1993) *Anti-Discriminatory Practice*. Basingstoke: Macmillan.

Thornton, P. and Lunt, N. (1995) *Employment for Disabled People: Social Obligation or Individual Responsibility?* York: Social Policy Research Unit Occasional Paper.

Thornton, P., Banks, P., Riddell, S. and Beyer, S. (2004) *A Study of Providers New to WORKSTEP*, Research Report W195. Sheffield: Department for Work and Pensions Research Management.

Tinker, A. (2009) ESRC & Technology Strategy Board Public Policy Seminar, Social and Behavioural Issues Influencing the Development and Adoption of Assisted Living Technologies. Presentation, September 11, London.

Tomlinson, S. (1982) *A Sociology of Special Education*. London: Routledge and Kegan Paul.

Tomlinson Report (1943) *Report of the Inter-Departmental Committee on the Rehabilitation and Resettlement of Disabled Persons.* London: HMSO.

Townsley, R., Abbott, D. and Watson, D. (2003) *Making a Difference? Exploring the Impact of Multi-Agency Working on Disabled Children with Complex Health Care Needs, Their Families and the Professionals who Support Them.* Bristol: Policy Press.

Turner M. (2000) *'It Is What You Do and the Way That You Do It'.* Report on user views on the introduction of codes of conduct and practice for social care workers by the four national care councils, commissioned from the Shaping our Lives User Group by the Office for Public Management, London.

Vernon, A. (2002) *User-Defined Outcomes of Community Care for Asian Disabled People.* Bristol: The Policy Press and Joseph Rowntree Foundation.

VODG (2007) *Response to the Green Paper on Adult Social Care from the Voluntary Organisations Disability Group.* London: VODG.

Walker, A. (1981) *Underqualified and Underemployed: Handicapped Young People and the Labour Market.* London: Macmillan.

Ward, D. and Mullender, A. (1993) 'Empowerment and Oppression: An Indissoluble Pairing for Contemporary Social Work', in J. Walmsley, J. Reynolds, P. Shakespeare and R. Woolfe (eds) *Health, Welfare and Practice: Reflecting on Roles and Relationships.* London: Sage.

Warren, J. (2005) 'Disabled People, the State and Employment: Historical Lessons and Welfare Policy', in A. Roulstone and C. Barnes (eds) (2005) *Working Futures: Disabled People, Policy and Social Inclusion.* Bristol: Policy Press.

Warner, L., Nicholas, S., Patel, K., Harris, J. and Ford, R. (2000) *Improving Care for Detained Patients from Black and Minority Ethnic Communities.* London: Sainsbury Centre for Mental Health.

Washington, J., Paylor, I. and Harris, J. (2000) 'Poverty Studies in Europe and the Evolution of the Concept of Social Exclusion', in J. Bradshaw and R. Sainsbury (ed.) *Researching Poverty.* Aldershot: Ashgate. pp. 263–83.

Wates, M. (1997) *Disabled Parents: Dispelling the Myths.* Radcliffe Medical Press and National Childbirth Trust.

Wates, M. (2003) *It Shouldn't Be Down to Luck: A Consultation with Disabled Parents.* Available at: www.DisabledParentsNetwork.org.uk

Weinberg, A., Williamson, A.J., Challis, D. and Hughes, J. (2003) 'What do Care Managers Do? A Study of Working Practice in Older Peoples' Services', *British Journal of Social Work,* 33: 901–91.

Whittam, J. (2007) Progressing the Single Assessment Process. Presentation: Centre for Policy on Ageing Event. Available at: http://www.cpa.org.uk/sap/sap_powerpointpresentations_list.html

Williams, V. and Holman, A. (2006) 'Direct Payments and Autonomy: Issues for People with Learning Difficulties', in J. Leece and J. Bornat (eds) *Developments in Direct Payments.* Bristol: Policy Press.

Wolfensberger, W. (1972) *The Principle of Normalization in Human Services.* Toronto: National Institute on Mental Retardation.

Woodin, S. (2006) *Mapping User-Led Organisations: User-Led Services and Centres for Independent Living.* London: Department of Health.

Young, A.F. and Ashton, E.T. (1956) *British Social Work in the Nineteenth Century.* London: Routledge and Kegan Paul.

Young, A., Temple, B., Davies, L., Parkinson, G., Bolton, J., Milborrow, W., Hutcheson, G. and Davis, A. (2006) *Early Support: An Evaluation of Phase 3 of Early Support*. DfES Research Brief RB 798.

Zarb, G. and Oliver, M. (1993) *Ageing with a Disability: What Do They Expect After All These Years?* London: University of Greenwich.

Zola, I.K. (1989) 'Towards the Necessary Universalizing of a Disability Policy', *Milbank Quarterly*, 47(Supp 2, Pt 2): 401–28.

List of legislation and statutory policy documents   ● ● ● ● ● ●

Audit Commission (2003) *Services for Disabled Children: A Review of Services for Disabled Children and their Families*. London: Audit Commission.

Audit Commission (2004) *Assistive Technology – Independence and Wellbeing Report No 4*. London: Audit Commission.

Cabinet Office (2005) *Improving the Life Chances of Disabled People*. London: Cabinet Office and Prime Ministers Strategy Unit.

CSCI and Health Care Commission (2009) *Commissioning Services and Support for People with Learning Disabilities and Complex Needs: National Report of a Joint Review*. London: Commission for Social Care and Audit Commission.

CSIP (2006) *Out and About: Wheelchair Services for Disabled Children*. London: Care Services Improvement Partnership and Department of Health.

CSIP (2007) *Getting to Grips with Commissioning for Services for People with Learning Disabilities*. London: Care Services Improvement Partnership and DH Social Care Programme.

DCSF (2008) (Bercow Report) *Better Communication: Improving Services for Children and Young People with Speech, Language and Communication Needs*. London: Department for Children, Schools and Families.

DCSF (2009) *Achievement for All*. London: Department for Children, Schools and Families.

Department of Constitutional Affairs (2007) Mental Capacity Act 2005 Code of Practice. London, DCA, TSO.

DfES (2001) Special Educational Needs (SEN) Code of Practice. London: TSO.

DfES (2004a) *Every Child Matters*. London: Department for Education and Skills.

DfES (2004b) 5 Year Strategy for Children and Learners. London, Department for Education and Skills.

DfES and DOH (2002) *The Early Support Programme: Professional Guidance*. London: TSO.

DHSS (1969) *Ely Hospital Enquiry Findings*. Department for Health and Social Security, London, HMSO. Available at: http://hansard.millbanksystems.com/lords/1969/mar/27/ely-hospital-cardiff-inquiry-findings (accessed 19/10/09).

DHSS (1969) *Ely Hospital Enquiry Findings*. Available at: http://hansard.millbanksystems.com/lords/1969/mar/27/ely-hospital-cardiff-inquiry-findings (accessed 19/10/09).

DHSS (1989) White Paper. *Caring for People*: Community Care in the Next Decade and Beyond (Cm. 849). London: HMSO.

DHSS and the Welsh Office (1971) *Better Services for the Mentally Handicapped*. London: HMSO.

DoH (1990) *Community care in the next decade and beyond*. Guidance document. London: HMSO.

DoH (1996a) Personal Social Services Direct Payments Order 1996. Statutory Instrument 1977: No 133 C6. London: DoH.

DoH (1998) *Modernising Social Services: Promoting Independence, Improving Protection, Raising Standards.* London: Department of Health.

DoH (1999a) *National Service Framework for Mental Health.* London: Department of Health.

DoH (1999b) HSC 1999/180: Ex parte Coughlan follow up action continuing health care follow up to the Court of Appeal judgement in the case of R. v. North and East Devon Health Authority. London, DoH. Available at: http://www.dh.gov.uk/en/Publicationsandstatistics/Lettersandcirculars/Healthservicecirculars/DH_4004718

DoH (2000): LAC 1. Community Care (Direct Payments) Amendment Regulations 2000. London, DoH.

DoH (2001a) *Valuing People: A New Strategy for Learning Disability in the 21st Century.* London: Department of Health.

DoH (2001b) *Health Survey for England.* London: Department of Health.

DoH (2002) *Planning with People – Towards Person-Centred Approaches – Guidance for Implementation Groups.* London: Department of Health.

DoH (2003a) *Fair Access to Care Services: Guidance on Eligibility Criteria for Adult Social Care.* London: Department of Health.

DoH (2003b) *Discharge From Hospital: A Good Practice Checklist.* London: Health and Social Care Joint Unit Change Agent Team. London: DoH.

DoH (2004a) *National Service Framework for Children.* London: Department of Health.

DoH (2004b) *Single Assessment Process for Older People.* London: Department of Health.

DoH (2004c) Draft Mental Health Bill. London, Department of Health.

DoH (2005a) *Independence Wellbeing and Choice: Our Vision for the Future of Social Care for Adults in England.* London: Department of Health.

DoH (2005b) *Building Telecare in England.* London: Department of Health.

DoH (2005c) *Improving Services for Wheelchair Users and Carers: Good Practice Guide.* London: Department of Health.

DoH (2006) *Our Health, Our Care, Our Say: A New Direction for Community Services.* London: Department of Health.

DoH (2007a) *Putting People First: A Shared Vision and Commitment to the Future of Adult Social Care.* London: Department of Health.

DoH (2007b) *Independence, Choice and Risk: A Guide to Best Practice in Supported Decision-Making.* London: Department of Health.

DoH (2007c) *The National Framework for NHS Continuing Healthcare and NHS-funded Nursing Care.* London: Department of Health.

DoH (2007d) *Mental Capacity Act Training Materials.* London: Department of Health. http://www.dh.gov.uk/en/Publicationsandstatistics/Publications/PublicationsPolicyAndGuidance/DH_074491

DoH (2007e) *Mental Capacity Act: Guidance.* London, Department of Health.

DoH (2008a) *Case for Change: Why England Needs a New Care and Support System.* London: Department of Health.

DoH (2008b) *Speech, Language and Communication Needs Action Plan.* London: Department of Health.

DoH (2008c) (Darzi Report) *High Quality Care for All: NHS Next Stage Review Final Report.* London: Department of Health.

DoH (2008d) *Personalisation Resources Toolkit.* London: Department of Health.

DoH (2008e) *The NHS in England: The Operating Framework for 2009/10.* London: Department of Health.

DoH (2009a) *Personalisation of Social Care Services.* London: Department of Health.

DoH (2009b) *Shaping the Future of Care Together.* London: Department of Health.

DoH (2009c) *Telecare Learning and Improvement Network.* London: Department of Health.

DoH (2009d) *Valuing people now: from progress to transformation - a consultation on the next three years of learning disability policy.* London, Department of Health.

DoH & DfES (2003) *Together from the Start - Practical Guidance for Professionals Working With Disabled Children (Birth to Third Birthday) and Their Families.* London: DoH and DfES.

DoH & DfES (2006) Options for excellence: Building the Social Care Workforce of the Future. London, Department of Health & the Department for Education and Skills. London, TSO.

DWP (2002) *Pathways to Work: Green Paper.* London: Department for Work and Pensions.

DWP (2005) *Five Year Strategy.* London: Department for Work and Pensions.

DWP (2009) *The Right Payments Programme.* Department for Work and Pensions. Available at: http://www.dwp.gov.uk/about-dwp/customer-delivery/disability-and-carers-service/dcs-news/ (accessed 19/10/09).

HM Government (1834) Poor Law (Amendment) Act.

HM Government (1990) National Health Service & Community Care Act: Statute. London: TSO.

HM Government (1995) Carers (Recognition and Services) Act. London: HMSO.

HM Government (1996) Community Care & Direct Payments Act: Statute. London: TSO.

HM Government (1999a) Disability Rights Commission Act: Statute. London: TSO.

HM Government (1999b) Health Act: Statute. London: TSO.

HM Government (2000) Carers and Disabled Children's Act: Statute. London: TSO.

HM Government (2001) Special Educational Needs and Disability Act: Statute. London: TSO.

HM Government (2003) Community Care Direct Payments (Scotland) Regulations: Statute. London: TSO.

HM Government (2004) Children Act: Statute. London: TSO.

HM Government (2005) Carers Recognition Act. London: TSO.

HM Government (2005) Mental Capacity Act. London: TSO.

HM Government (2006) National Health Service Act: Statute. London: TSO.

HM Government (2008) Welfare Reform Act: Statute. London: TSO.

HM Treasury and DCSF (2007) *Aiming High for Disabled Children: Better Support for Families.* London: Department for Children, Schools and Families.

Office of the Deputy Prime Minister (2000) *Building Regulations Part M.* London: TSO.

Office for Disability Issues (2008) The United Kingdom Advisory Network for Disability Equality (Equality 2025) First report December 2006–June 2008

Office for Disability Issues (2008) *Independent Living Strategy.* London: ODI. Available at: http://www.officefordisability.gov.uk/docs/wor/ind/ilr-summary.pdf (accessed 19/10/09).

OFSTED (2006) HMI 2535: 'Inclusion: Does It Matter Where Pupils Are Taught?' Available at: http://www.ofsted.gov.uk/Ofsted-home/Publications-and-research/Browse-all-by/Education/Inclusion/Special-educational-needs/Inclusion-does-it-matter-where-pupils-are-taught/(language)/eng-GB (accessed 4 August 2009).

PMSU (2005) Improving the Life Chances of Disabled People. A joint report with Department of Work and Pensions, Department of Health, Department for Education and Skills, Office of the Deputy Prime Minister. DWP, DoH, DfES and ODPM. London, TSO.

Scottish Government, (2009) Personalisation: A Shared Understanding Commissioning for Personalisation A Personalised Commissioning Approach to Support and Care Services Edinburgh, Changing Lives Service Development Group.

Scottish Parliament (2008) *Free Personal and Nursing Care. 4th Report of the Scottish Parliament's Audit Committee.* Edinburgh: Scottish Parliament.

SCIE (2008) *Co-Production: An Emerging Evidence Base For Adult Social Care Transformation.* SCIE Research Briefing 31. Available at: http://www.scie.org.uk/publications/briefings/briefing31/index.asp (accessed 19/10/09).

SSI (1999) *Recording with Care: Inspection of Case Recording in Social Services Departments.* London: Social Services Inspectorate & Department of Health.

Index